In 1929, when the Warsaw Convention containing certain rules relating to international carriage by air was drafted, charter operations were very rare in the field of aviation. The question of the applicability of the Warsaw Rules to air charter was therefore intentionally left open. Nowadays charter operations form a substantial part of air transportation. Thus, we are now forced to seek a solution of the important problem whether or not the Warsaw Rules are applicable to air charter agreements.

In this book, the problem of interpretation just mentioned has for the first time been discussed in detail. The book may be useful for all those who are interested in air law or engaged in air charter operations. It may also be of current interest from an international legislative point of view, as the problems concerning hire and charter of aircraft are now on the agenda of the Legal Committee of ICAO.

Air Charter and the Warsaw Convention

AIR CHARTER

AND THE WARSAW CONVENTION

A Study in International Air Law

By KURT GRÖNFORS

LL.D., Assistant Professor
University of Stockholm

Springer-Science+Business Media, B.V.

PUBLISHED WITH THE SUPPORT OF THE

Swedish Social Science and Legal Research Council

Originally published by Almqvist & Wiksel/Stockholm in 1956.
Softcover reprint of the hardcover 1st edition 1956

Almqvist & Wiksells Boktryckeri AB

UPPSALA 1956

ISBN 978-94-017-6699-9 ISBN 978-94-017-6762-0 (eBook)
DOI 10.1007/978-94-017-6762-0

PREFACE

This study deals with a problem which is of practical importance chiefly to air carriers and may therefore seem to be highly specialized. But it may also be looked upon as a modest contribution to one particular aspect of an ever-fascinating general problem in legal theory—that of the effect of mandatory rules.

Much of the material was collected during a stay in the spring of 1954 at the Institute of International Air Law, McGill University, Montreal. My research work in this world center of civil aviation organization was made possible mainly thanks to an invitation by Professor John Cobb Cooper, who was then the Director of the Institute. I should like in this place to express my gratitude to Professor Cooper for the kind and generous interest he has taken in my work.

I also want to acknowledge the generosity of the Sweden-America Foundation, as well as of the Edvard Cassel Foundation, University of Stockholm.

For inspiring discussions and valuable information I am much indebted to several foreign experts in air law and to a number of Swedish friends.

January, 1956.

K. G.

CONTENTS

INTRODUCTION

In 1929, when the Warsaw Convention containing certain rules relating to international carriage by air[1] was drafted, the type of contract known as charter contract (charter agreement) was very rare in the field of aviation. Although the question as to the applicability of the Convention to air charter was raised at the Warsaw Conference, it was intentionally left open.[2] The reason was that charter operations were not yet sufficiently developed and clarified. Since that time the situation has completely changed. Nowadays charter operations form a substantial part of air transportation and they show an increasing tendency to become more important.

One result of this evolution is that we now are forced

[1] For the full text of this Convention, see *infra*, Appendix A.

[2] *II Conférence Internationale de Droit Privé Aérien, 4–12 Octobre 1929, Varsovie,* Warszawa 1930 (Imprimé et publié par les soins du Ministère des Affaires Étrangères de Pologne), pp. 97, 216–217. Cf. Coquoz, *Le droit privé international aérien,* Paris 1938, pp. 90, 279; Riese, *Luftrecht,* Stuttgart 1949, pp. 408–409; Ambrosini, *Noleggio e trasporto aereo,* Nuova rivista di diritto commerciale, diritto dell'economia, diritto sociale 1952, pp. 224 et seq., on p. 225; Alten, ICAO Doc. 7450-LC/136, p. 130; Litvine, *Précis élémentaire de droit aérien,* Bruxelles 1953, No. 177 (p. 133); and Drion, *Limitation of Liabilities in International Air Law,* The Hague 1954, No. 118 (p. 133).

to seek a solution of the problem whether or not the Warsaw Rules are applicable to air charter agreements. This problem of interpretation has special significance owing to the fact that, according to Article 23 of the Convention, any provision in a contract of carriage tending to relieve the carrier of liability or to fix a lower limit than that which is laid down in the Convention is declared to be null and void. The rules of the Convention are, in this sense, mandatory. In other words, the Warsaw Convention can be described as the Harter Act of air carriage. It is thus necessary to decide the scope of the Convention as exactly as possible, in order to make it clear which types of contracts are outside the Convention and are consequently ruled by the principle of contractual freedom (naturally, within the limits that are fixed by the national law). Hence, the question of the applicability of the Warsaw Convention is a basic problem for the whole law of air charter contracts. It is this question that will be discussed in the following pages.

The problem can, of course, be attacked in many different ways and with the use of various methods of interpretation. As an example, it may be mentioned that a common law judge and a civil law judge might come to rather different conclusions merely because of their way of approaching legal problems.[3] As, according to the British view, a common law

[3] Cf. Hughes, *Problems of Liability Arising from the Chartering of an Aircraft* [unpublished manuscript], (Institute of International Air Law, McGill University), Montreal 1952, pp. 15 et seq. – This and other manuscripts here quoted are term papers, available in the Library of the Institute of International Air Law, McGill University, Montreal. Although not published, they offer too much of interest to be excluded from the material discussed in this study. It may here be pointed out that the quotations from these papers are made in full consciousness

judge, at least in principle, is not allowed to take into account the discussions which took place when the Convention was being drawn up, but can only try to interpret the intention of the legislature from the words of the Convention itself, he would probably find that most charter operations are "international carriage" within the meaning of Article 1, provided that the geographical conditions are satisfied, and are therefore also covered by the Convention. A civil law judge, on the other hand, might base his interpretation on the above-mentioned fact that the problem concerning the applicability of the Warsaw Convention to charter contracts was intentionally left open, and for some reason reach the conclusion that such operations need not be covered by the Convention. Therefore, no solution of the problem here dealt with can be expected to become unanimously recognized as internationally valid. Every judge must regard the problem with the law of his own country as a background, and because of this the results obtained may differ considerably.

For this reason, the following analysis does not pretend to supply a complete answer to the problem or to provide the rationale for "the only correct solution". Its purpose is, rather, a more modest one—to contribute to the solution by trying to outline and justify the opinion that the author holds to be the most reasonable one, taking into account all the circumstances that are relevant according to his opinion. That the solution recommended must be tentative is also a necessary consequence of the fact that, so far as the author knows, the problem has been the subject neither of exten-

of the possibility that the authors might not consent to the publication in full of the papers in their present form.

sive studies nor of any important court decisions. The author has tried to compensate to some extent for the lack of material by inquiring into the opinion of some leading legal advisers in the field of air transportation business and also by examining various model charter agreements with a view to getting an idea of the actual structure of the air charter business. In order to obtain a solution that has any chance of being approved by lawyers representing different legal systems, the author has tried to derive his arguments mainly from the Convention itself—thus concentrating upon arguments of which the importance has in fact already been internationally recognized.

Chapter I THE CONCEPT OF CHARTER CONTRACT

The concept of charter contract[1] was originally developed in the field of maritime law.[2] It is usual to make a rough distinction between the three following types of maritime charter contracts, of which only two are considered as "real" charter agreements:—

(1) Voyage charter agreements, i.e. agreements concerning the chartering of an equipped ship (ship with crew) for one or more determined voyage or voyages.

[1] Cf. with this chapter Grönfors, *Några anmärkningar rörande charterbegreppet i lufträtten* [Some Remarks concerning the Concept of Charter in Air Law], Beiträge zum internationalen Luftrecht (Festschrift für Alex Meyer, Verkehrswissenschaftliche Veröffentlichungen Heft 32), Düsseldorf 1954, pp. 50 et seq. (With a Summary in German.)

[2] The principal source of knowledge about maritime charter in English law still seems to be Scrutton's famous book on *Charterparties and Bills of Lading,* 16th ed. by Lennox McNair & Mocatta, London 1955. For American law, see Poor, *American Law of Charter Parties and Ocean Bills of Lading,* 4th ed., New York 1954. Cf. by the same author *Informal Lectures on Charter Parties and Bills of Lading,* [Isbrandtsen-Steamship Co., Inc.] New York [1944]. See also Cooley, *Chartering and Charter Parties,* New York 1947. Problems arising out of a typical maritime model charter agreement have been recently discussed at length by Rørdam, *Treatises on the Baltcon-Charterparty,* London 1954.

(2) Time charter agreements, i.e. agreements concerning the chartering of an equipped ship for a specified period of time, the particular voyages to be determined later on by the charterer.

(3) Bare-hull (bareboat) charter or demise charter agreements (charter by demise), i.e. agreements concerning the "chartering" of a non-equipped ship.

The last type of charter contract (3) is in fact a lease of an "empty" ship and has therefore, it is said, more in common with the rules relating to lease of property than with the other two types of charter agreements. As to these, it is often pointed out that frequently they are not clearly distinguishable. In practice one can find elements of both voyage charter and time charter in the same agreement, and the circumstances are therefore in fact usually not so simple as those described above. It is, for example, common to charter an equipped ship for one or more determined voyage or voyages but nevertheless to pay a charter price fixed on a time basis. The main line of distinction is often said to be found in the method of calculating the charter price (the hire). If the price is fixed on a time basis, the agreement is looked upon as a time charter agreement; if the price is fixed on a voyage basis, the contract is considered to be a voyage charter agreement.

From the survey of various doctrines given in Ch. III, we shall find that many authorities have in fact used the concepts of voyage charter, time charter and bare-hull charter in the same or nearly the same sense as the corresponding terms are used in maritime law. Nevertheless, it may, with respect, be doubted whether one can possibly reach well-founded results merely by transferring these maritime law concepts to the field of air law.[3] The technical and economic structure of air charter business differs indeed on important points from that of maritime charter.[4] The effective transport time is shorter, the method of handling the goods is quite different, the quantity of goods that can be carried in the transport vehicle is much smaller, the purpose of the charter arrangement may be different, etc. Maritime charter agreements mostly concern the carriage of goods, but air charter agreements very often cover only the transportation of passengers and their luggage. In maritime charter agreements the particular ship is mostly individualized by its name, while, in air charter agreements, it is quite usual to specify the type of aircraft only, thus leaving open the question of which particular aircraft is to perform the charter flight. Other differences can also be found, but the points now mentioned seem to be the most important ones.

It would, to take only one example, be most impractical to build up air charter rules on the presupposition that a distinction should be made between time and voyage charter, as those concepts are interpreted above. In air transportation, the charter price is often fixed through a combination of various charges.[5] Some of these may be calculated on a time

[3] As to the whole question of the applicability of maritime law concepts and rules to air law, see Grönfors, *Om trafikskadeansvar* (On liability for damage to third parties, caused by ships, railways, motor vehicles and aircraft), Stockholm 1952, pp. 356 et seq., with further references.

[4] Cf. Serraz, *De l'affrètement aérien et de certains rapports juridiques qui en découlent,* Revue générale de l'air 1949, pp. 349 et seq., especially p. 351.

[5] According to the *Pan American World Airways System Charter Contract,* para. 2, the charter price is to be fixed by cumulating a mileage charge, ferry charge, layover charge, excess valuation charge on

basis and others on a voyage basis. Now and then the situation may be so complicated that one cannot possibly decide how to classify the agreement.

Airplane charterers usually pay a basic charge, called a mileage charge, based on the distance flown. Although the usual way of measuring airplane operations is by the number of flight hours, these are always "translated" into flight miles, the common standard of distance; for it is easier to construct an appropriate customer's price with this latter standard as the starting point. The reason why the charter price is not fixed at a certain amount of money per day, week etc., the charterer being free to use the airplane for this period of time as little or as much as he wants, is said to be the comparatively short time in which an airplane becomes worn out. It is therefore necessary in air charter business, as distinguished from shipping, to examine in detail the exact number of operating hours. Airplane owners usually settle at least the leading features of the planned voyages beforehand, thus giving some sort of maximum limit for the number of effective flight hours allowed within the scope of

baggage or cargo, insurance charge, all taxes payable in respect of the charter flight or transportation sold thereon, and certain expenses. The *KLM Royal Dutch Airlines Aircraft Charter Agreement* provides in Article 5 that the charter price "shall include the cost for fuel, oil and maintenance of the Aircraft, landing fees, parking fees, hangar fees, ground service and dispatch costs for the Aircraft, salaries, flight pay and per diem of the crew, and the costs of the service for passengers during the flights and during their stay on the ground at the intermediate stations, on the basis of the service usually extended by KLM to the passengers in flight and at these stations; provided that where an intermediate stop would exceed 72 hours only, the service costs for the first 72 hours only shall be included in the Charter Price unless the delay is due to negligence of KLM". In Article 1 there is a space left for specifying both the route and the duration of the journey.

the air charter agreement. If making a mileage charge a main part of the charter price were considered to constitute, at least in principle, a calculation of the charter price on a voyage basis, this would mean a plain denial of the existence of time charter in the field of air transportation (except for the rare cases where the charter price depends *directly* on the number of flight hours). And this in spite of the fact that the measurement that is decisive for airplane operations is in reality the number of effective flight hours. This example shows that purely technical circumstances can lead to unexpected results when maritime law concepts are applied to air law.

These are some of the reasons why it seems insufficient to base the following study on parallels and analogies from maritime law. Another reason that may be stated is the different construction in most countries of the liability rules in maritime law and air law respectively.[6] For example, from a historical point of view the Warsaw Convention has, in many respects, been influenced more by the Berne Convention on Railway Transportation than by the Hague Rules. And the problem of the scope of these latter Rules, especially insofar as they require the issuing of a bill of lading, is decidedly different from the question of the applicability of the Warsaw Rules. Insofar as the Hague Rules allow the parties to agree upon exclusion or limitation of the carrier's liability or upon extension of his rights, the common method of contracting out of the Rules is to issue no bill of lading; omission to issue an air consignment note (air waybill) has,

[6] One exception is the Italian *Codice della navigazione, 1942.* The main idea behind this statute is that maritime law and air law are indivisible. Concerning the *Codice* and the so-called Naples School, see e.g. Cacopardo, *Das Luftrecht im neuen italianischen Codice della navigazione,* Archiv für Luftrecht 1943, pp. 34 et seq.

as we shall find later on, quite a different legal effect, viz. that of depriving the carrier of his right to avail himself of those provisions of the Warsaw Convention which exclude or limit his liability. In consequence, the bare non-existence of the required transportation documents can only according to the Hague Rules, and never according to the Warsaw Rules, be considered as a fact indicating that the carriage falls outside the scope of the Rules.

It seems obvious that the subject here dealt with can be properly attacked only from an "air law" angle. This, of course, does not mean that air law should be separated from other branches of transportation law, or that parallels would be of no interest.[7]

In the air transport industry, the term "charter" is used in a very wide sense, meaning *at least all carriage relating to the usage of non-scheduled services.*[8] In one of the charter agreements examined the term seems to have an even wider meaning: the airline company agreed to undertake the transportation between New York and Copenhagen of 48 passengers in a DC-6 aircraft, furnished for the disposal of the charterer, whereas the remaining 11 passengers of the group in question were to be carried on the airline's usual scheduled service on this route.[9] Even though the word "charter" was not used in the agreement, this was clearly looked

[7] The maritime charter rules may, to take only one example, be of great importance when dealing with the problems concerning the charter price in air law.

[8] Cf. Krüger, *Der Begriff der "Charter" im Luftverkehr,* Flugwelt 1954 No. 1, pp. 7 et seq.

[9] Draft Agreement Nov. 1949 between *Federazione tra le associzione del clero in Italia (FIDAT)* and *Scandinavian Airlines System (SAS),* para. 3.

upon by the airline company as a charter contract, although transportation on a scheduled air service was also involved. Perhaps they considered the combining element of the voyages, i.e. the character of the transportation as a group transportation of passengers, as the deciding factor. The reason would be that in such cases ("group of passengers", "consolidated shipments") the price could be based on a special calculation. Furthermore, a typical voyage charter agreement may also provide for a considerable number of regular voyages on a certain route, each voyage to be carried out according to a fixed timetable—a situation which seems to be properly characterized as a scheduled air service.[10] It is necessary, however, to make the reservation that the exact meaning of the term "scheduled service" is not quite clear.[11] Finally it may be mentioned that special flights with tasks other than that of performing transportation, e.g. aerial photography or crop dusting, are sometimes called and sometimes not called charter flights.

From a legal point of view, however, it seems impracticable to use the vague concepts, such as "voyage" or "time",

[10] e.g. Agreement of September 15, 1952, between *Fred Olsens Flyselskap A/S* and *SAS*. Now and then a charter contract covers only one or two voyages, which are to be carried out according to a fixed timetable. See e.g. Agreement of January 4, 1951, between *AB Nordisk Resebureau* and *SAS*. In such cases there seems to be no reason to compare the flights to the scheduled ones.

[11] For a definition, see ICAO Doc. 7278-C 841, 10/5/52, cf. ICAO Doc. 7576-C 880. Cf. Alex Meyer, *Der internationale Luftlinienverkehr und der international entgeltliche Gelegenheitsverkehr nach geltendem Recht und de lege ferenda unter besonderer Berücksichtigung einer Koordinierung des europäischen Luftverkehrs,* Zeitschrift für Luftrecht 1954, pp. 223 et seq. See also Schenkman, *International Civil Aviation Organization,* Genève 1955, pp. 333 et seq.

"scheduled" or "non-scheduled", that have been described. These concepts cover so many different types of contracts which have very little in common. Therefore it is quite natural that most authors dealing with air charter should have tried to evolve a more sharply defined concept. They have often started by excluding some groups of charter contracts, e.g. for logical reasons or because of the "nature" of the contract, and in this way have from the very beginning restricted the area covered by their study.[12] But it must be admitted that such a method involves certain risks. It may be that some types of contracts are excluded from the analysis without satisfactory reasons, or at least that in this way part of the "total picture" of the problems relating to air charter is obscured. In order to avoid such a result, we shall in this study take the term "charter contracts" in its widest sense. Only such operations as aerial photography and crop dusting are left aside. The possibility of creating a sharper and more practical concept is a terminological question that can only be answered when the examination has been completed and so offers a basis upon which to solve this problem.[13]

Before we try to sharpen the contours of our problem of interpretation, we might briefly describe the contents of a typical air charter agreement. For a survey of the contents seems in itself to give at least an impression of the ordinary type of contract here in question and thus constitutes a useful background for the analysis which follows.

It is probably of no interest to try to distinguish only the

[12] For some examples of suggested definitions, see the previously mentioned article by Grönfors, pp. 53–54 (with critical comments).

[13] See *infra*, Conclusion.

very few characteristics that might be common to all air charter agreements, as some of these agreements are made out individually and are very thoroughly adapted to the special circumstances of the actual case in view. Other agreements, however, are—either completely or with some minor exception—in conformity with some model charter agreement prepared by an airline or a trade organization. Examples of both types of contracts have already been mentioned in the footnotes to this chapter. In order to find a more extensive group of typical provisions we need only consider the standard air charter agreements of leading air carriers.

Such agreements often contain some four or more pages of detailed rules and regulations.

They start by giving the names of the parties and the company's promise to charter to the other contracting party a fully manned and equipped airplane, specified by identification letters or otherwise, or, more commonly (as has already been mentioned), an airplane of a specified type (e.g. DC-6, Constellation), equipped and manned with a licensed crew but not further individualized. In this connection there are often included other particulars, referring to the aircraft and the way it has to be used by the charterer, e.g. particulars concerning the chartered space, maximum load capacity and seating accommodation under the agreement, types of cargo permitted, etc.

These provisions are followed by a description of the proposed journey. This includes at least a specification of the places of departure and destination and also of the date or dates of the flight. Usually, however, the agreement also specifies the time for embarking and loading as well as the duration of the journey. Sometimes a detailed flight schedule with all agreed stopping places is included.

The charter price is, as stated above, usually fixed through a cumulation of various charges. Often the parties have also agreed upon the demurrage rate and cancellation fee, the method of payment, the currency valid for payment under the agreement, the distribution between the parties of various expenses (e.g. landing, parking and hangar fees), etc.

All the provisions now mentioned form together the part of the contract through which the latter is individualized. In the printed forms space is always left for filling in the specifications. But as a rule the other conditions are fixed beforehand in the model agreement and not modified from case to case (with the only exception that it is always possible, if necessary, to include special provisions in the standard agreement). These conditions concern a great many subjects, the most important of which are the issuance of transportation documents, the non-performance or partial performance of the journey, the resale of chartered space and the liability under which the carriage is performed. Some specimens of clauses on these subjects will be mentioned and discussed later on in this study.

Chapter II THE TWO MAIN PROBLEMS

The parties to an air charter agreement are the *airplane owner* and the *charterer*.

The former is the person who is the owner of the airplane according to the national laws of property. In some countries the owner is the person who is officially registered as the owner by the authorities, while in other countries such a registration is irrelevant.

Sometimes the term "owner" seems to be too narrow, for even a person who is not the owner may be able to conclude a charter contract just as if he were the owner. If, for example, a charterer does not use the complete transport capacity of the aircraft, he can sell the space available to another person, the *sub-charterer,* provided that the resale of chartered space has not been restricted.[1] The charterer then,

[1] Members of International Air Transport Association (IATA) are bound by the special provisions in "Resolution 045" concerning the resale of chartered space, extracts from which are given *infra,* Appendix B. The adoption of this resolution has led to special clauses in the standard charter agreements. See, for an example, the *Pan American World Airways System Charter Contract,* para. 10: "The Charterer hereby represents, warrants and agrees that he has not already held out and will not hold out by advertisement, course of conduct or other means, individual passages to the public generally for transportation on the charter trip. ..." If this stipulation is violated, the Company, according to para. 11, has the right to cancel the contract immediately

in fact, in relation to his sub-charterer, plays a rôle similar to that of the owner in relation to the charterer. For the sake of convenience the special case of sub-charter is not as a rule covered in the following,[2] but generally the same rules and arguments seem to be applicable.

In some cases the charterer is a *passenger* or *shipper (consignor),* and the airplane owner his *carrier.* It is, however, a common situation that the passenger or shipper is not identical with the charterer but is a person *outside* the charter agreement. A few examples will make this clear. An airline company charters from another company an airplane with crew in order to meet a sudden increase of the transport demand on one of its regular routes. Or a travel agency charters an equipped aircraft and then sells the space individually. Accordingly, the problem of the applicability of the Warsaw Convention in such cases must be divided into two main problems:—

(1) Is the Convention applicable to the charter agreement, i.e. to the contractual relationship between the airplane owner and the charterer?

(2) If there is someone other than the charterer who is able to insist on being covered by the Convention—whether he be a passenger or a shipper outside the charter agreement—is it the airplane owner or the charterer who is responsible according to the rules of the Convention? Or are they, perhaps, both subject to these rules and responsible, either jointly or jointly and severally?

and, in the event that the charter flight has commenced, to terminate the flight at any time, all without liability of any kind to the charterer or any member of the group on behalf of which the charter is made.

[2] For an exception, see *infra,* Ch. V (11).

Having thus divided, in principle, our problem of interpretation, we have to clear up the relationship between the two main problems. Are they quite separate or are they interrelated? Is it proper to take into consideration the solution of the first problem when trying to solve the second one?

In order to find the correct answer to these questions we may start from an uncomplicated example. A charters an equipped airplane (i.e. an airplane with licensed crew) to B, and B sells the space, either the whole of it or part of it, to C. If the charter agreement between A and B falls entirely outside the scope of the Warsaw Rules, this circumstance naturally does not exclude the application of the Convention to the contractual relationship between B and C. But let us consider the opposite solution, that the Warsaw Rules are supposed to apply to the charter agreement between A and B. In such a case it might be appropriate to treat C in the same way as B and thus apply the same set of rules to both contracts. This method would mean a practical coordination of the claims and responsibilities created by the same incident. But this argument can never be decisive, as the application of the Warsaw Rules to the contractual relationship between B and C is not a necessary consequence of the application of the same rules to the contractual relationship between A and B. The connection here pointed out between the two problems is only a practical one, and the argument can do no more than add one reason—and perhaps a not very important one—to other possible reasons for the same solution.

The effect of the application of the Warsaw Rules to both contracts can also be described as follows. If the charter agreement between A and B is covered by the Convention, it seems to make no difference as far as the final result is concerned whether C is given the right to sue B or the right to sue A direct (provided that A and B are both solvent and that B has not by contract accepted a more extended liability). For B, having been sued by C, must always have the possibility of suing A, relying upon the same mandatory rules as C. The problem of which one is the *carrier, stricto sensu,* and thus responsible according to the Convention *in relation to C* does not seem, in these circumstances, to be very important. But the solution of this problem has an indisputable influence on the final result, if the Warsaw Rules are to be considered not applicable to the charter agreement between A and B. In such a case B, having been sued by C, has no possibility of suing A on equal terms, as the contractual relationship between A and B follows only the provisions in their agreement and the rules of the national law. If these rules are not as far-reaching as the Warsaw Rules, the person deemed to be responsible as carrier within the meaning of the Convention will in reality bear the whole burden or the major part of it. And if there exists a possibility for B to sue A according to the agreement or the national law, A might not have the advantage of a limitation of his liability, corresponding to the limits according to the Convention, which would be applicable if C were allowed to direct a claim against A, based on the Warsaw Rules.

From this it may be clear that there is, on the one hand, no necessary connection from a logical point of view between the two main problems of interpretation but, on the other hand, some connection from a practical point of view. This connection means that the final result of the incident causing the damage, as regards the liability, might be different in different cases and in consequence the solution of the first problem might influence the solution of the second. This is why both problems will be dealt with in the following analysis. Only such a broad perspective can be expected to give a correct impression of the impact of the Warsaw Convention on air charter transportation.

The following study about the applicability of the Convention to contracts between airplane owners and charterers, i.e. about the first of the two main problems here discussed, is naturally based upon the assumption that the parties have not by agreement extended the scope of the Convention. The author thus presupposes that the parties have not put into their agreement anything about the applicability of the Convention, or that they have declared the Warsaw Convention applicable to the carriage "only insofar as the same is governed thereby",[3] or that they have excluded the applicability of the Warsaw Rules[4]—this last provision

[3] This is the case in *Baltairpac,* para. 10. There it is further stated that "in all other cases Owners accept no liability whatsoever for death, injury or delay of passengers or loss or damage to or delay of their baggage during the flight or any transport to or from Airfields of departure or destination or any intermediate Airfield or elsewhere".

[4] Cf. the *Air France Contrat d'affrètement passagers et bagages,* Article VI:

1. Indépendamment des dispositions du présent contrat, le transport effectué en exécution de ce dernier sera régi par les Conditions Générales de Transport Passagers et Bagages de la Compagnie AIR FRANCE [cf. the following footnote], dont un extrait figure au verso des titres de transport et qui sont tenus à la disposition du public dans ses bureaux et agences.
2. Plus spécialement, il est convenu que la Compagnie AIR FRANCE sera dégagée des obligations contractées par elle, et que sa responsabilité ne pourra être mise en cause si, par suite d'un évènement de force majeure, tel que conditions météorologiques inter-

perhaps being inconsistent with the mandatory character of these rules and in such cases lacking any legal effect.

In all these cases, the question as to the applicability of the Convention has not been influenced by the parties, and thus we have to answer the question by means of legal interpretation.

However, it is not uncommon in air charter business to-day that the owner and the charterer agree that the Warsaw Rules shall apply to the contract, even if this would not have been automatically governed by the Convention.[5] Such clauses, which may here be called *Warsaw Clauses*, exist in

disant l'envol ou obligeant à dérouter l'avion, grève, actes de gouvernement et autres faits semblables échappant à son contrôle, ainsi que par suite de pannes mècaniques ou avaries, elle était empêchée de procéder au transport qu'elle s'est engagée à effectuer, ou si celui-ci devait être différé ou subir un retard en cours de route, ou encore si le lieu de destination prévu devait être modifié.

Dans un pareil cas AIR FRANCE ne pourra être tenue à autre chose qu'au remboursement de la partie du prix de l'affrètement correspondant à la partie du parcours non effectué. AIR FRANCE toutefois, fera tout son possible pour acheminer à leurs frais passagers et bagages jusqu'à leur lieu de destination finale.

3. En cas de divergence entre les dispositions des conditions générales de Transport Passagers et Bagages et celles contenues dans le présent contrat, ce sont ces dernières qui prévaudront.

[5] A common method is to declare the companies' General Conditions of Carriage applicable to carriage under the charter agreement. And these General Conditions are usually founded on the Warsaw Rules. See for examples of such a method the *British Overseas Airways Corporation Special Flight Order Agreement,* para. 3, the *KLM Royal Dutch Airlines Aircraft Charter Agreement,* Article 12, and the *SABENA Contrat de transport d'un groupe de passagers (de transport de marchandises),* para. 3. Cf. Ambrosini, *op. cit., supra,* Introduction, footnote 2, pp. 235–236. See also Rhyne, *Aviation Accident Law,* Washington 1947, p. 258.

many different wordings. Generally speaking, the rules of the Convention are then extended beyond their ordinary limits. Anyhow, we can only reach a more detailed description of the real legal effect of Warsaw Clauses after completing the whole analysis of our problems of interpretation.[6] For such an analysis seems to be necessary as a background for a correct description.

[6] See *infra,* Ch. VI.

Chapter III PREVIOUSLY SUGGESTED METHODS FOR DECIDING THE APPLICABILITY OF THE WARSAW RULES TO AIR CHARTER

It now seems desirable to outline briefly the various methods that have been suggested for solving our problems of interpretation and to examine the arguments presented. Even though these problems have not yet been much discussed, such a critical survey of what has actually been said can be expected to supply a valuable basis for further analysis.

The methods here discussed cannot possibly be arranged quite satisfactorily from a logical point of view. The reason for this is that they have not been constructed to fit into a closed logical system. In consequence, there is nothing left to do but arrange the material in a way that seems, from a practical point of view, convenient with regard to our purpose. We shall start by discussing the opinion that the Warsaw Convention never applies to charter agreements (1), and shall finally reach the directly opposite view that the Convention always applies to such agreements but for one distinct exception (6). Between these two extremes we will group various methods of interpretation, all of them resulting in a partial application of the Convention (2–5).

Some authors referred to in this chapter discuss both of the main problems of interpretation at the same time. Others seem to have only one of the problems in mind, and as a rule the first one (i.e. whether or not the Convention applies to the contractual relationship between the airplane owner and the charterer). As far as can be judged from the material here presented, they usually do not try to distinguish explicitly between the two questions. Sometimes it may even be difficult to know for certain whether they intend to deal with both of the interrelated problems, or with only one of them. Hence, it seems appropriate, and in some cases even necessary, to keep both problems in sight when discussing previously suggested methods for deciding the applicability of the Warsaw Rules to air charter. But when the two main problems of interpretation come to be analyzed more closely in the next chapter, they will be clearly separated in order to avoid confusion.

(1) One view of the problem here dealt with might be that *the Warsaw Convention never applies to charter agreements.* This seems to be the opinion of Belardinelli[1] and of Kaiser.[2]

[1] Belardinelli, *Contratto di noleggio e contratto di trasporto in relazione alla Convenzione di Varsavia del 12 Ottobre 1929,* Rivista di diritto aeronautico 1933, pp. 129 et seq. As to his reason for this opinion, see *infra* (4) *in fine.* Some statements by Gay de Montellá, *Principios de derecho aeronáutico,* Buenos Aires 1950, pp. 389 et seq., seem to indicate a similar interpretation.

[2] Kaiser, *Der Personenbeförderungsvertrag im Luftrecht,* Diss. (Erlangen), Würzburg 1936, pp. 92—93: "Für den Chartervertrag im Luftrecht interessiert besonders die Frage, ob dieser unter das WA. fällt oder ob dieses hier unanwendbar ist. Diese Entscheidung hängt davon ab, ob eine der Parteien des Charterungsvertrags als Luftfrachtführer im Sinne des WA. anzusehen ist." "... beim Chartervertrag niemals eine der Parteien Luftfrachtführer nach WA. ist. Auch z. B. nicht in den Fällen, wo Goedhuis das Abkommen für anwendbar erklärt. Wird in einem solchen Fall der Charterer selbst eine bestimmte Strecke be-

They both find it conclusive that the Convention, according to its own wording, covers only "contracts of carriage" and that a charter agreement never constitutes such a contract, although it does constitute an obligation with the main purpose of putting an equipped airplane at someone's disposal. Under these circumstances they regard none of the parties to such a contract as a carrier within the meaning of the Convention. The Norwegian Judge Alten has argued along the lines that the Convention only mentions the "carrier" as the responsible person, not the "owner" of the airplane or the "charterer".[3] This way of reasoning, however, is highly formalistic and conceals the difficult problem whether the owner or the charterer can be deemed to be a carrier within the meaning of the Convention and the charter agreement is thus equivalent to a contract of carriage.

A similar, though not quite identical, point of view has been argued by Hesse, who cannot find any convincing reason for applying the Convention to air charter contracts, although certain charter operations might, having regard to the wording of the Convention, be considered subject to the same

fördert, so geschiet dies auf Grund des Chartervertrags. Der Hauptzweck ist das Zurverfügungstellen des Luftfahrzeugs, nicht die Beförderung. Andernfalls ist eben kein Charterungsvertrag, sondern ein Beförderungsvertrag gegeben, auf den dann das WA. Anwendung finden muss. In der Ablehnung einer Ausdehnung des Geltungsbereichs des WA. auf den Chartervertrag des Luftrechts gehen wir einig mit Belardinelli, der vor allem aus dem Wortlaut des WA., das nur von einem 'contratto di trasporto', nicht von einem 'contratto per il trasporto' spricht, darauf schliesst, dass das WA. nur auf den eigentlichen Beförderungsvertrag in der Luft angewendet werden kann." As to the opinion of Goedhuis here referred to, see *infra* (3).

[3] Alten, Citeja Doc. 336, p. 10. If this be the correct interpretation of Alten's rather vague and very short statement on the subject, Alten has apparently changed his view since; see *infra* (4).

Convention.[4] Ambrosini may have been thinking very much on the same lines, as he finds it certain that the Convention does not apply to what he calls "real" charter, and especially not to time charter.[5] In a later article, however, he points out that standard voyage charter agreements have usually been given the character of contracts of carriage and that, as such, they are covered by the Convention.[6]

Of the writers now mentioned, Hesse has expressed his view the most thoroughly. His main arguments may be summarized as follows.

There seems to be no need to restrict the freedom of contract in the field of charter operations. The Warsaw Convention is a typical "common carrier" Convention, having the aim of protecting the public from what Hesse calls "wanton dictation of the conditions of carriage". As the passengers or consignors are not united or are not able to unite into as strong a bargaining group as the airlines, there would, without this protection, be a risk of too many exceptions and limitations of the carriers' liability. Such a motive for the protection of passengers or consignors cannot be found in the field of charter operations. "The charterer usually chooses the charter party, because he is a large shipper, in an economically strong position to bargain for himself. He can and will insure his goods and is usually well versed in the business of carriage himself. He does not require

[4] Hesse, *A Paper on the Problems of Liability Arising from Charter-parties in Air Law* [unpublished manuscript], (Institute of International Air Law, McGill University), Montreal 1952, pp. 25–32.

[5] Ambrosini, *Fletamento y transporte (con relación al llamado "charter" aviatorio),* [mimeograph] Buenos Aires [1951], p. 3.

[6] See pp. 236–237 of this article, referred to *supra,* Introduction, footnote 2. Cf. *infra,* Ch. VI.

protection from the law... If he wants protection from the law he can still select to carry his goods or himself under an airwaybill and ticket respectively, thus enjoying the protection at his will and need."[7]

Besides, a "charterer" is neither a passenger nor a consignor in the legal meaning of the terms; he is a party *sui generis,* not provided for in the Convention.[8]

It thus appears to be very much in doubt whether the text of the Convention is meant to cover charter operations. This seems to be the case not only in situations where the charterer intends to fly himself or carry his own cargo but also where he decides to sublet the space of the aircraft wholly or in part to others or to carry for others. "The cases either come both within the scope (of the Convention) or not at all."[9]

Hesse's basic argument—lack of need of protection—may be important in many cases of charter operations. Nevertheless, Hesse seems to have underestimated the widespread use of air charter today. It is, in fact, possible to find a great many charter agreements where the charterer has just the same inferior position in relation to the owner as an ordinary passenger or consignor in relation to the carrier.[10]

As to the other arguments, Hesse seems to some extent to

[7] Hesse, *op. cit.*, pp. 22, 29. Cf. e.g. Hughes, *op. cit.*, p. 16; Riese, Citeja Doc. 336, p. 16; Alten, ICAO Doc. 7450-LC/136, p. 130; and Drion, *ibid.*, p. 132.

[8] Cf. Alten's opinion, as referred to above.

[9] Hesse, *op. cit.*, p. 26.

[10] e.g. transports of displaced persons when the charterer is a private person as representative for the group of persons demanding transportation, or transports of groups of tourists when the charterer is a small travel agency. In cases where the charterer is in a financially weak position, it is usually stipulated that the charter price must be paid in good time (one week or more) before the actual start of the flight.

have overlooked other difficulties that arise here. The charterer may in fact appear in some situations as the carrier within the meaning of the Warsaw Convention, as we shall see later on. And we shall find cogent reasons for adopting the method of breaking down the relations in charterparties which is criticized by Hesse.[11]

On the whole, Hesse's standpoint, as well as that of the other authorities just mentioned, must be characterized as too restrictive, as it does not seem to give full credit to the mandatory character of the Warsaw Rules. Hesse is obviously aware of this himself, for—in spite of his own more restrictive interpretation—he concludes by stating that "under the Warsaw Convention certain charter-operations might be considered subject to this Convention eventually, limited in scope arising from the construction of the term 'passenger' and 'consignor' or of article 34 or otherwise by interpretation . . .".[12]

(2) It might be possible to apply the Warsaw Convention to *all situations where one of the parties (the owner or the charterer) appears to be the carrier in the sense that he controls the crew and, therefore, the technical execution of the carriage.* The French authors Coquoz and de Juglart seem, like the Belgian author Litvine, to take such a standpoint,[13] and the same idea may, to some extent, be the base for some

[11] See *infra* (3).

[12] Hesse, *op. cit.*, p. 32. Incidentally, it seems likely that, by "eventually", Hesse meant "possibly".

[13] See Coquoz, *op. cit.*, p. 92; de Juglart, *Traité élémentaire de droit aérien*, Paris 1952, No. 276 (p. 326); Litvine, *op. cit.*, No. 180 (p. 134). As to the standpoint of Coquoz, see further *infra* (3) and (6).

arguments put forward by Shawcross & Beaumont.[14] According to a statement by Beaumont, this standpoint seems to be reasonable.[15] If this interpretation is accepted, the term "carrier" would be almost identical with the term "operator".[16]

The authorities arguing this principle of interpretation seem to have chiefly the second main problem in mind, i.e. the question of who has the status of carrier in relation to passengers and shippers, but the wording sometimes also covers the first main problem, that concerning the relationship between the aircraft owner and the charterer.

One reason for the standpoint here dealt with might be that, as Litvine points out, according to Article 30 of the Warsaw Convention, referring to successive transports, the carrier need not be a person who was also a party to the contract of carriage. But the same argument might equally well be used as an *argumentum e contrario*. Because the case of successive transports is specially mentioned, the Convention would be supposed to base itself, without any other exception, upon the principle that the carrier must be a party to the contract of carriage. In fact, this latter argumentation

[14] Shawcross & Beaumont, *Air Law,* 2nd ed., London 1951, No. 512 (ii), 513(C), 513(D).

[15] Beaumont, ICAO Doc. 6014, LC 111, 16/8/48, p. 124. As to what appears to be the personal view of Beaumont on the problem *de lege lata,* see *infra* (4).

[16] For a contrary interpretation, see e.g. Alten, ICAO Doc. 7157-LC 130, p. 11: "The charterer did not have the use of the aircraft and was not an operator. While the operator had complete use of the aircraft, the charterer had only a personal claim against the operator to have transport carried out."

seems to be more in conformity with the construction of the Warsaw Rules.[17]

There are also other reasons which militate against the solution now discussed.

As regards non-contractual damage (to third parties on the surface) it would be reasonable to consider a charterer who himself or with his own crew operates the airplane to be the responsible person.[18] One of the purposes of the rules of liability is to stimulate precautionary measures which, of course, cannot be taken by anyone other than the person who in fact supervises the operation of the aircraft. The situation in the case of contracts of carriage, however, is somewhat different. The main point here is that the passenger or consignor has concluded a contract with one person or undertaking. If there is nothing specially agreed, expressly or implicitly, about the way of carrying out the obligation, the latter party might perform the transport himself or he might use others (whom he would be well advised to choose with great care, as he is responsible for their execution of the transport). From the passenger's or consignor's point of view, the question of who in fact controls the technical execution of the transport might not be so important alone in providing the basis for deciding the question of the applicability of the Warsaw Rules. For passengers and consignors may, above all, want freedom to choose their contractual party and debtor.

One of the main difficulties connected with the principle of interpretation which we are now discussing is the follow-

[17] Cf. the result gained by Drion, *op. cit.*, No. 124 (p. 142).

[18] Cf. the Rome Convention 1952, Article 2.

ing. The principle permits the carrier to contract out of the Warsaw liability at any moment he wishes by merely using another operator, perhaps a financially weaker one, without the passengers or consignors even knowing it. This seems to weaken considerably the privilege granted to passengers and consignors by giving the Warsaw Rules mandatory character.

Finally, this method of interpretation would result in a very wide application of the Convention and for that reason involve the risk of forcing the Warsaw Rules on situations for which they are not adapted. This last argument will now be studied further.

(3) One method of deciding the application of the Warsaw Rules to air charter contracts might be to use the test that it *must be possible to consider the charterer as a passenger or consignor within the meaning of the Warsaw Convention.* This test has been suggested by Goedhuis.[19] When carefully examined, however, his argumentation is seen to be much more complicated than that. Goedhuis' discussion is undoubtedly one of the most important contributions to the problem and it will therefore be reproduced here. Briefly, his argument is as follows.

[19] Goedhuis, *Les contrats de charte et de louage des aéronefs en connexion avec la Convention de Varsovie du 12 Octobre 1929,* Revue de droit international et de législation comparée 1932, pp. 687 et seq., especially p. 690 *in fine.* See also the following works by the same author: *La convention de Varsovie,* La Haye 1933, pp. 92 et seq., and *National Airlegislations and the Warsaw Convention,* The Hague 1937, pp. 131 et seq. As to Goedhuis' later position, see *infra* (5). Cf. Cogliolo, Citeja Doc. 288, p. 3: "... l'affrêteur n'est certainement pas un simple voyageur et c'est pour cela qu'il ne rentre pas dans le terrain specifique de la Convention de Varsovie."

One premise is that it can be concluded from the text that the Convention only considers the regulation of the *direct relation between the person or undertaking that concluded a contract of carriage on the one hand and the passengers or consignors with whom the contract was made on the other.*[20]

[20] Of the same opinion are, e.g., Wulff, *Die Haftung des Lufttransporteurs im nationalen und internationalen Privatrecht,* Diss. (Hamburg), Würzburg 1938, pp. 18–19; van Houtte, *La responsabilité civile dans les transports aériens intérieurs et internationaux,* Louvain & Paris 1940, No. 77 (p. 123); Jost, *Der Haftpflichtprozess in der Schweiz,* Bern 1951, p. 125; Schleicher & Reymann, *Recht der Luftfahrt,* 2nd ed. 1937 reprinted, Berlin & Köln 1954, p. 348; and Schweickhardt, *Schweizerisches Lufttransportrecht,* Zürich, Berlin & Köln 1954, pp. 50–51. Cf. McPherson, *Air Charter* [unpublished manuscript], (Institute of International Air Law, McGill University), Montreal 1952, pp. 17–18, who on the same grounds comes to the conclusion that "a time or voyage charter is a contract of carriage but not one that would fall within the jurisdiction of the Warsaw Convention". Shawcross & Beaumont also seem in one statement, *op. cit.,* No. 362 note (a), to consider the directness of the relation between the parties as decisive, but they use a different argument. They say: "In view of the decisive importance given by Art. 1(2) to 'the contract made by the parties', it is submitted that this is the governing factor, and that, in respect of each passenger or consignor, 'the carrier' means the person who has contracted with him for the carriage." Cf. the comment as to this point by Riese, reviewing one of Goedhuis' books in Archiv für Luftrecht 1934 p. 47: "Es wird Aufgabe des Gerichts sein, je nach Lage des Einzelfalles festzustellen, wer Luftfrachtführer ist. Auszugehen ist dabei von dem auch vom Verf. anerkannten Grundsatz, dass Luftfrachtführer i. S. des Abkommens stets derjenige ist, der es vertraglich übernimmt, Reisende, Gepäck oder Frachtgut mit einem Luftfahrzeug zu befördern." As to the concept of carrier in German law, cf. Abraham, *Die Grade des Verschuldens des Luftfrachtführers in ihrer Auswirkung auf seine Haftung aus Beförderungsverträgen,* Zeitschrift für Luftrecht 1955, pp. 255 et seq., on p. 258: "Luftfrachtführer ist derjenige, der sich im *eigenen* Namen zur Beförderung von Personen, Gepäck oder Gütern auf dem Luftwege verpflichtet. Ob er diesen Vertrag mit einem Flugzeug, dessen Halter er

A carrier who, owing to the very mode of transportation, is unable to fulfill the requirements of the Convention as to the drawing up of transportation documents—which can be done only by a carrier in direct relation to passengers or consignors—cannot be considered as a carrier within the meaning of the Warsaw Convention. Since the absence, irregularity or loss of the transportation documents has, according to the Warsaw Rules, the effect of depriving the carrier of the right to avail himself of those provisions which exclude or limit his liability—Articles 3 (2), 4 (4), 5 (2) and 9—and thus is in a way punitive, it would be unreasonable to make persons unable to issue the required documents subject to the Convention. For this reason the abovementioned test has to be combined with the principle that *the owner, charterer or sub-charterer must be able to issue the necessary documents* in order to be in a position to avail himself of those provisions which exclude or limit his liability. Only in this case can he be *considered to be a carrier within the meaning of the Convention.*

From his discussions of some special types of air charter it becomes obvious that Goedhuis actually adds to his two principles a third: *the charter contract must be of a construction that permits determination whether or not the carriage is international within the meaning of Article 1 of the Convention.*[21] If such determination is impossible, the Convention can never apply, as in order to answer the ques-

gleichzeitig ist, oder ohne Haltereigenschaft erfüllt, ist regelmässig gleichgültig."

[21] Of the same opinion are, e.g., Koffka, Bodenstein & Koffka, *Luftverkehrsgesetz und Warschauer Abkommen*, Berlin 1937, p. 269, and Wulff, *op. cit.*, p. 19. Cf. Hughes, *op. cit.*, p. 18.

tion of its applicability in the first place the transportation must be qualified as international.

With these three principles as a basis for the discussion, Goedhuis arrives at the conclusion that air charter carriage comes under the Warsaw Rules only in a comparatively few cases.

Bare-hull charter (hire or lease of a non-equipped aircraft) never does, because such a charter cannot be considered as a contract of carriage, i.e., in the terms of Goedhuis, the owner is not a carrier within the meaning of the Convention. If, however, the charterer concludes contracts of carriage with passengers and consignors he must be considered as a carrier within the meaning of the Warsaw Convention, and this carriage will thus be governed by this Convention.

Nor, according to Goedhuis, do time charter agreements (where the owner puts an equipped airplane at the disposal of the charterer for a certain specified time, and the charterer can determine the journeys to be made) usually fall within the scope of the Convention. If the charterer is a private individual who wishes to make an undetermined journey, it is impossible to qualify the carriage as international and the owner cannot issue the required transportation documents before the departure; for these reasons the Warsaw Rules are not applicable.[22] If the charterer, instead, concludes contracts with passengers or consignors, the charterer in this relation becomes a carrier within the meaning of the Convention, which is thus applicable. But precisely the opposite situation meets us regarding the contract between the owner and the charterer; this is not a contract of carriage. In other words,

[22] The same opinion is held by Maniatopoulos, Citeja Doc. 423, p. 17.

the owner is not a carrier within the meaning of the Convention.

The Warsaw Rules, Goedhuis states, apply to a wider extent to voyage charter agreements (where the owner puts at the disposal of the charterer an airplane equipped to make a specified journey which is international within the meaning of the Convention). If the charterer is a private individual who himself wishes to make the journey or who wishes to carry his own merchandise, the owner should be regarded as a carrier within the meaning of the Warsaw Convention, "because the carriage is international and for reward,[23] and because the charterer can be considered as a passenger" (or consignor).[24] This carriage therefore comes under the Convention.[25] If the charterer concludes contracts of carriage with passengers or consignors, the charterer in this situation will also be deemed to be a carrier within the meaning of the Convention, which thus applies. The owner, however, cannot in his relation to the charterer be looked upon as a carrier, as he is unable to satisfy the obligations of a carrier to issue the required transportation documents (no direct relation between him and the passengers or consignors).

The general idea behind the three leading principles of Goedhuis seems to be that *the Warsaw Rules cannot apply if, because of their construction, they do not fit properly into the charter situation in question* (i.e., the situation does not

[23] This statement does not seem to be strictly correct, as even gratuitous carriage *by an air transport undertaking* is covered by the Warsaw Convention. See Article 1 (1).

[24] Goedhuis, *National Airlegislations,* p. 134.

[25] The same opinion is held by Maniatopoulos, Citeja Doc. 423, p. 4.

lend itself to the Rules).[26] It must be clearly stated that this argument is a very strong one. But it is, of course, necessary to prove that the Rules cannot in fact be adapted to the charter situation at hand. In this respect Goedhuis' interpreting methods and results have been criticized by Coquoz.[27]

In the case of time charter, the obligation to issue transportation documents may appear formalistic but at any rate would not be impossible for the owner to carry out. In fact, it is not unusual in air transportation that the owner issues special tickets or consignment notes direct to passengers or consignors, even if these have previously contracted with the charterer.[28] The issuance of such passenger tickets would be especially easy if one group ticket for all passengers (instead of a separate ticket for every passenger) were generally considered to meet the requirements of the Convention.[29] As to the irregularity of the passenger ticket, the absence of one or more of the required particulars does not influence the ability of the carrier to avail himself of those provisions which exclude or limit his liability; Article 3 (2). Of the particulars required under sanction in luggage tickets, only those of the number and weight of the packages would cause some slight trouble; Article 4 (3 f). The difficulty of deciding whether the transport is to be deemed international within the meaning of the Convention, while not realized by the authors of the Convention, is a fact which should apparently, according to Coquoz, be taken into consideration when in-

[26] Cf., for a similar idea, Schonfeld, Citeja Doc. 313, p. 3.

[27] Coquoz, *op cit.*, pp. 96, 98.

[28] Cf. Shawcross & Beaumont, *op. cit.*, No. 362 note (a).

[29] Drion, *op. cit.*, No. 252 (pp. 300–301), finds that the issuance of one group ticket would in certain circumstances be allowed by the Convention.

terpreting the Convention. Anyhow, this difficulty could perhaps be overcome in practice, if one tried to answer the question separately for each flight within the scope of the charter agreement. In all cases where transportation documents have been issued, the text of these will quickly solve the problem. For, as Sack has very clearly put it, the "test of applicability of the Convention is the character, not of the *voyage* made (or to be made) *by the aircraft,* but of the *transportation* contracted by, or for, the given subject (passenger, baggage, merchandise)".[30]

It cannot be denied that these critical comments reveal a weakness in Goedhuis' argument. Nevertheless, they do not fully achieve their object, which is to show that the Warsaw Rules can be made to apply to practically all kinds of air charter without serious difficulty. On the contrary, it must be admitted that at least the air consignment note particulars set out in Article 8 (g)–(i)—namely the nature of the goods, the number of the packages, the method of packing and the particular marks or numbers upon them, the weight, the quantity, the volume or dimensions of the goods—may cause serious trouble. This has not been mentioned by Coquoz. But, on the other hand, there is nothing in the Warsaw Convention that forces the carrier to issue the transportation documents at the same time as he concludes the contract of carriage. As Hürzeler has pointed out,[31] the carrier can issue the documents later, i.e. just before the departure of every single flight within the scope of the charter agree-

[30] Sack, *International Unification of Private Law Rules on Air Transportation and the Warsaw Convention,* Air Law Review 1933, pp. 345 et seq., on p. 350. (Italics by Sack.)

[31] Hürzeler, *Probleme des Chartervertrags nach Luftrecht,* Diss. Zürich 1948, p. 28.

ment,[32] and at this time it is *as a rule* possible to fill in all the required particulars. But not in all cases. If, for example, the charterer himself is responsible for the loading of the plane—which is perhaps not common but is nevertheless a situation that arises in airline practice[33]—it may be virtually impossible for the airplane owner to take any measures in order to secure the above-mentioned particulars. The owner might not, in this and in other charter situations, be very successful in convincing the charterer that he is in fact a consignor within the meaning of the Convention, and therefore has to make out an air consignment note and hand it over, with the goods, to the owner as carrier; Articles 5 (1) and 6 (1).[34] And it is undoubtedly ridiculous to require, in accordance with Article 6 (3), the owner (carrier) to sign on acceptance of the goods by charter transports in cases where he has never "accepted" any goods.

As a general remark it may here be added, that the carrier cannot possibly escape the loss of his liability limits by intentionally filling in fictitious particulars without having obtained the necessary pieces of information about the true nature of the goods etc. The sanction certainly does not seem applicable if one or more of the required particulars have

[32] If the goods were received at an earlier moment but it was impossible to have the air consignment note made out even at the moment of acceptance, the carrier has the possibility of offering a simple receipt, containing part of the information necessary. Cf. the mate's receipt in maritime law. Drion, *op. cit.*, No. 262 (p. 307).

[33] See e.g. *Baltairvoy 1951*, clause 6 (i) and (ii).

[34] But in some contracts it is an express condition that the charterer must prepare air consignment notes, supply the owner with all documents whatsoever and wheresoever required in respect of the cargo, and indemnify the owner for any inaccuracy, omission, or non-completion. Thus *Baltairvoy 1951*, clause 6 (v).

by chance been incorrectly stated, but if the carrier intentionally fills in the wrong statement he might, on the contrary, be said to have accepted the goods without the consignment note containing all the prescribed particulars and thus to be unable to avail himself of those provisions which exclude or limit his liability.[35] And, so far as the author can see, the intentional filling in of wrong information is equivalent to the formal filling in of fictitious information merely in order to preserve the liability limits. Both cases are incompatible with the rationale of the provisions requiring such detailed transportation documents, i.e. the importance of having access to *reliable* pieces of information about the goods carried, in case of an accident.

As a summary of the arguments discussed above, Goedhuis must be said to have clearly shown that some of the Warsaw Rules are, if not quite impossible, at least practically impossible or not very well adapted for application to some typical charter situations.

(4) Some authorities, dealing with the problem of the applicability of the Warsaw Convention to air charter, have based their decision on the question *whether or not the charter agreement at the same time involves an obligation to carry*. Contrary to the writers previously mentioned, who completely deny the possibility that the type of contract known as charter agreement can ever be qualified as a contract of carriage,[36] the authorities here dealt with hold that the mere existence of an obligation to carry is enough to turn a charter contract into a contract of carriage falling

[35] Drion, *op. cit.*, No. 271 (pp. 311–312).

[36] *Supra* (1).

within the scope of the Convention. Their main reason for this opinion is that the Warsaw Convention, according to its Article 1, refers to all contracts on international air "carriage" and that it must therefore be considered to cover all such contracts, even those charter agreements that involve the obligation just mentioned. Representatives of this opinion are Hürzeler,[37] Riese[38] and Drion,[39] and probably also Beaumont[40] and Alten.[41]

[37] Hürzeler, *op. cit.*, pp. 27–29.

[38] Riese, *Luftrecht,* Stuttgart 1949, p. 408. Cf. the same author in Citeja Doc. 297, p. 10; 336, p. 11. See also Riese & Lacour, *Précis de droit aérien,* Paris 1951, No. 284 (p. 235) and Abraham, *Der Luftbeförderungsvertrag,* Zeitschrift für das gesamte Handelsrecht und Konkursrecht 117 (1954/55), pp. 82 et seq., on pp. 103–104 (extended reprint, Stuttgart 1955, pp. 25–26). Cf. the following statement (with no special reference to charter agreements, however) by Moller, *The Law of Civil Aviation,* London 1936, p. 294: "In the same way in the carriage of goods by air the test, as to the applicability or otherwise of the Warsaw Rules, centres primarily upon the nature of the contract of carriage and whether the contract governs what is an international carriage within the Rules." Here may also be quoted the following passages by Hughes, *op. cit.*, pp. 22–23: "On one point, however, most of the authorities seem to agree—namely that the only person covered by the Convention as it now stands is the person with whom the passenger or shipper has a contract of carriage. Thus where A charters an aircraft to B, and B enters into a contract of carriage with C, then although the persons who operate and navigate the aircraft are the servants of A, yet it is B, and B alone, who is the 'carrier' within the meaning and for the purposes of the Convention." The general correctness of this statement, which has no exception, is respectfully doubted for reasons given in this book. In fact, Hughes seems to have mixed up two arguments, namely that concerning the obligation to carry and that of directness in relation between carrier and passenger/consignor (in the name of which person were the transportation documents issued?).

[39] See *infra* in the text.

[40] Beaumont, *Need for Revision and Amplification of the Warsaw Convention,* The Journal of Air Law and Commerce 1949, pp. 395 et

Against this point of view one objection has been made by Hesse. According to him, this would at least be contrary to practice under the common law of the British Commonwealth and of the United States: in both systems a charterparty containing an undertaking to carry is still a charterparty.[42] If the idea of an obligation to carry as an essential part of the charterparty (thus qualifying this as a contract of carriage) were just another way of expressing the previously mentioned principle that the owner must be a carrier within the meaning of the Warsaw Rules, Hesse's argument could not possibly have any reasonable meaning. For the latter principle is undoubtedly quite in line with legal thinking in common law. It is thus necessary to answer the question whether the two methods now referred to are identical or not.

The answer to this question can perhaps best be found by giving an example of a practical charter situation. A travel agency charters an airplane for a voyage on a certain route. The agency then individually sells the whole capacity of the plane to tourists and issues under its own name passenger and baggage tickets to each one of these. In this case it cannot be doubted that there is no direct contractual relationship between the owner of the airplane and the passengers. For that reason the owner would not, according to the previously mentioned principle (Goedhuis), be deemed

seq., on p. 412: "... in the second case [sc., when the charterer himself employs space in the chartered aircraft in carriage for remuneration], the charterer becomes a 'carrier' because he himself makes a contract to carry." French translation in Revue française de droit aérien 1950, p. 168. Cf. Chauveau, *Droit aérien,* Paris 1951, No. 472 (pp. 240–241). See also *supra* (2).

[41] Alten, ICAO Doc. 6027 LC/124, p. 60. Cf. *supra* (1).

[42] Hesse, *op. cit.,* p. 14.

to be a carrier. But does the charter agreement between the travel agency and the owner of the plane involve an obligation to carry? The answer will most probably be Yes, and using this test the owner would be qualified as a carrier. The two theories seem in such a case to lead to different results and Hesse's argùment will then be quite understandable.

But we cannot be quite sure that the answer will be affirmative. And here we are facing a difficulty which affects the whole idea of the obligation to carry as the test of the applicability of the Convention. Almost every charter agreement that is not a plain bare-hull charter contains an element, more or less obvious, of an (express or implied) obligation to carry. The question therefore is, how strong this element should be in order to allow the qualification of a charter agreement as a contract of carriage. If one uses this test for deciding the applicability, the line of distinction between Warsaw charters and "free" charters must be a very vague one. And there is yet another factor of uncertainty: has the judge to interpret the intention of the two contracting parties in question or shall he base his decision on the outline structure of the charter situations in question?

Drion has suggested in detail a method for deciding the question whether or not a certain charter agreement is to be deemed to involve any "obligation to carry".[43] His argument deserves attention as an effort to show how the "obliga-

[43] Drion, *op. cit.*, Nos. 53 and 120 (pp. 57–58, 136–138). Sidenbladh seems to be opposed to Drion's opinion as regards the position of the aircraft owner in case of time charter. See Sidenbladh's review of Drion's book, Svensk juristtidning 1955, p. 493.

tion to carry" theory as a test for the applicability of the Convention should be handled in practice.

He starts by declaring as a condition for the application of the Convention that the contract must be a contract of carriage, and one of carriage between agreed points. This excludes not only bare-hull charter but also time charter agreements. "A *voyage charter* [agreement], however, by which one person assumes the obligation to carry with his aircraft and crew, from one point to another, certain persons or goods agreed upon or to be indicated by the charterer, would be a contract of carriage governed by the Convention, even if not all persons or goods were to be embarked or off-loaded at the same points, since nothing prevents persons from agreeing in one contract on the carriage of passengers or goods over various stretches."

In relation to passengers and shippers the aircraft owner can be a carrier only if he has concluded a contract of carriage with respect to the persons or goods in question. "Any contract by which he has undertaken to carry the persons or goods from one agreed point to another will be sufficient for this purpose. The fact that an entire aircraft is reserved for such carriage does not deprive the contract of its character of a contract of carriage, nor the operator of his status of carrier within the meaning of the Convention. Nor is it essential that the persons or goods to be carried be determined at the moment the contract is concluded. Even with the normal contracts of carriage it may easily happen that a shipper contracts for the transportation of goods which he has still to buy."

Drion then illustrates his thesis by giving the following two examples. If a travel agent charters an equipped airplane for a tourists' trip between New York and Paris but issues transportation documents mentioning himself as carrier, both he himself *and* the aircraft owner would be qualified as carrier within the meaning of the Convention. For *the aircraft owner also would have concluded a contract of carriage* for the transportation of the persons between the agreed points. The situation would be the same when the charter contract concerns transportation of goods: the charterer would be a carrier because he had concluded contracts of carriage with the shippers, and the operator would be a *carrier because of his contract with the charterer.*

As far as can be concluded from these statements, a directness of relationship between the owner on the one hand and the passengers or shippers on the other would not, contrary to the opinion of Goedhuis (3), be necessary. Even an obligation directed to the charterer only and containing a promise to carry persons or goods not even specified would be quite sufficient. This vagueness of the "obligation to carry" requirement seems to make it possible to presume the existence of such an obligation in almost every case.

One exception, however, has been expressly mentioned by Drion. He states that "the operator who has given his aircraft and crew in time charter to another person has not, *by the execution of that time charter,*[44] concluded a contract of carriage with respect to the person or goods for whose transportation the charterer happens to use the chartered aircraft." But nothing, Drion continues, prevents the operator from concluding additional contracts of carriage by issuing tickets or consignment notes for persons and goods carried under the time charter agreement. Whether such an

[44] Italics by Drion.

issuance will amount to the conclusion of additional contracts of carriage or only be considered as a mere administrative formality will, according to Drion, depend on *the intentions of the parties*. In other words, the parties are free to decide whether they want to place themselves outside or inside the scope of the Convention, and this in spite of the fact that the Warsaw Rules are mandatory. This very result—that a set of rules having mandatory character and thus a legally defined scope independent of the intentions of the contracting parties is nevertheless found to depend for its application on the intentions of the parties—seems to indicate that there is something wrong with the method of interpretation recommended.[45]

The whole method seems to be somewhat over-subtle and impracticable, and it leads to rather unexpected consequences. It should therefore, if possible, be avoided. The method might also, as shown above, include a risk of so wide an application of the Convention to charter agreements that the Warsaw Rules are forced upon situations that, because of their construction, they may not be adapted to govern.

Curiously enough, the same method has proved also to be a suitable basis for quite a contrary result, viz. a very restricted application of the Warsaw Rules to charter agreements. According to Cogliolo, the rapporteur on this subject to the Citeja (Comité International Technique d'Experts Juridiques Aériens) before World War II, the Convention certainly applies to charter contracts which are really con-

[45] A matter apart is that, according to Article 1 (2), the applicability of the Convention also depends on the international character of the transportation and that this follows from the route contracted by the parties. Naturally, the parties must be free to choose the route of the journey.

tracts of carriage,[46] but charter agreements of this kind could only be found in cases of sub-charter. He expressly denies that the charter of a fully equipped aircraft can ever be considered as a transport agreement.[47] As has already been mentioned,[48] Belardinelli and Kaiser even go one step further. According to them, no charter contract can ever be deemed to be a contract of carriage.[49] It seems rather strange that what is basically the same principle can lead—or at least can be used so as to lead—to such extremely different results.

(5) As a matter of fact, it would perhaps be possible to decide the applicability of the Warsaw Convention by investigating *whether the owner or charterer has issued the transportation documents.*[50] As pointed out just above, the borderline between charter agreements on the one hand and contracts of carriage on the other can be extremely vague. It might clear up the situation if the decisive point were allowed to be the bare existence of such documents.[51]

[46] Cogliolo, Citeja Doc. 328, pp. 4–5; Doc. 336, pp. 6 and 15.

[47] Cogliolo, Citeja Doc. 336, p. 7: "En ce qui concerne les parties contractantes, il est evident que la Convention de Varsovie ne peut pas s'appliquer à la location d'un aéronef qui n'est pas loué armé. On ne peut même pas l'appliquer aux aéronefs armés mais livrés complètement à l'affrêteur. Il n'y a que le cas où il y a eu location d'une partie seulement de l'aéronef; alors, nous avons le contrat de transport. ... Mais lorsqu'il s'agit de la location d'un aéronef armé, avec la possibilité de voyager pendant un certain temps, d'aller où on veut, il ne s'agit plus d'un contrat de transport. Il s'agit alors d'une location *totius rei.* ..." Cf. *ibid.*, p. 16, and Citeja Doc. 328, pp. 4–5.

[48] *Supra* (1).

[49] Belardinelli, *op. cit.*, 132–133, 140–141; Kaiser, *op. cit.*, pp. 92–93.

[50] Cf. Hughes, *op. cit.*, p. 2.

[51] Cf. Hesse, *op. cit.*, p. 21 *in fine;* and also the United States Circuit court of Appeal in *Curtiss-Wright Flying Service, Inc.* v. *Glose*, 1933 U.S.

Nevertheless this standpoint is unacceptable, and this is so because of the text of the Convention itself. For it is quite clear that the absence or loss of a passenger ticket, luggage ticket or air waybill does not affect either the validity of the contract or the applicability of the Convention; the sanction is instead that mentioned above, i.e. the carrier is no longer entitled to avail himself of those provisions of the Convention which exclude or limit his liability; Articles 3 (2), 4 (4), 5 (2) and 9. *If* the required transportation documents are issued, the person or undertaking who issued them generally appears to the passenger or consignor as the carrier, and the Warsaw Convention seems to be applicable in this (direct) contractual relation.[52] And here we apparently meet a rather important aspect of our problem. But in cases where no transportation documents are issued, the problem still remains unsolved. The question that then arises can be put in this way: is this agreement a contract of the type that requires the documents described in the Warsaw Convention? This question can naturally be answered only on the basis of other facts than the mere existence of transportation documents. In *some* cases, however, it might be practical to use a test very much like the one now being dealt with, namely the following: *would it, from a practical point of view, be possible for the owner or charterer to issue Warsaw docu-*

Av. R. 26: When a ticket is issued, containing terms and conditions that clearly evidence the relation of passenger and carrier, the contract cannot be deemed to be a charter agreement.

[52] This is the leading idea upon which are based the remarks by Goedhuis, *Handboek voor het luchtrecht,* 's-Gravenhage 1943, pp. 207 et seq. Goedhuis seems thus to have somewhat changed his position as to the problem of interpretation here dealt with. Cf. *supra* (3).

ments? As shown above,[53] only if the answer is found to be affirmative is it reasonable to regard the contract as being within the scope of the Convention.

It should here be added that the test now mentioned—the existence of required documents—may not in some cases be quite so easy to apply as might at first sight appear, but may on the contrary give rise to certain difficulties.[54] How much is required for the documents to be recognized as having been issued? In the case *Fosbroke-Hobbes* v. *Airwork, Ltd., and British American Air Services, Ltd.,*[55] the tickets had been handed over in an envelope just before the start, but the plane crashed soon after take-off, before the recipient had any opportunity of seeing the contents of the envelope. Goddard J. (as he then was) said: "On these facts it seems to me impossible to hold that there had been a communication of the conditions of the hirer before the journey started, and an acceptance of them, express or implied, by him."

(6) The exact opposite of the viewpoint first described (1), would be the opinion that *the Warsaw Convention always applies to all kinds of charter agreements with the important exception of bare-hull charter.*[56] This is, in fact, the opinion of Coquoz. His thesis is that the Convention, according to Article 1, covers all international carriage that is not

[53] See *supra* (3).

[54] See Shawcross & Beaumont, *op. cit.*, No. 406 note (b).

[55] 1938 U.S. Av. R. 194 (High Court of Justice, King's Bench Division), also reported, *inter alia,* in [1937] All E. R. 108.

[56] No authority seems to have argued that a mere bare-hull charter is to be considered as falling within the scope of the Convention.

clearly intended to be excluded.[57] His arguments have been briefly mentioned above (3). Such a broad interpretation seems, even more than in the case of some of the other methods, to involve the risk of forcing the Warsaw Rules on situations in which, because of their construction, they do not fit very well. This must probably be deemed a serious objection to the thesis of Coquoz.

[57] Coquoz, *op. cit.*, pp. 90–93, 96, 98. Cf. Mateesco, *Droit aérien-aéronautique*, Paris 1954, p. 224.

Chapter IV AN ANALYSIS OF THE TWO MAIN PROBLEMS

Our critical survey of the discussion on the applicability of the Warsaw Convention has revealed a most confused picture. The opinions stated include nearly everything from a plain denial of applicability to the standpoint that the Convention applies to all air charters except bare-hull charter. Many reasons for one view or another have been found justifiable at least to some extent, while others appear less convincing. But no recommended method of interpretation has been found entirely satisfactory. The task now will be, on the basis of the above discussion and other relevant circumstances, to examine the problems of interpretation more closely.

(1) All the different methods described above have one premise in common, namely that the Warsaw Convention can apply only to cases where all the conditions of this Convention are satisfied. This is the natural starting point. It means, for instance, that the carriage may neither be performed by way of experimental trial by air navigation undertakings with a view to the establishment of a regular airline, nor in extraordinary circumstances outside the normal scope of an air carrier's business; Article 34. And the

carriage must be international within the meaning of Article 1 (2). This has never been doubted. The disagreement begins when we investigate the exact meaning of the condition that the agreement must concern a transport or that the responsible person must be the carrier.

It would be meaningless to apply rules concerning carriage by air to air charters if the circumstances in these two cases had no, or only very few, characteristics in common. Therefore the question arises whether contracts of carriage and charter contracts in air law do in fact show any major differences in their general structure.

The basic difference may be briefly described in this way. The contract of carriage represents the sale and purchase of *transportation of persons or goods,* i.e. an obligation to carry passengers or goods from one place to another. The charter contract relating to a fully equipped airplane represents the sale and purchase of *moving space,* i.e. an obligation to fly the airplane (loaded or not loaded) from one place to another. This situation may be characterized as containing elements of both carriage (transportation) and lease.[1] Finally, a bare-hull charter represents nothing but the mere *demise* of a "flight instrumentality" for use according to certain conditions.

This last case has obviously very little, if anything, in common with the first one, the sale and purchase of transportation. The transportation case and the moving space

[1] This mixture is neither a peculiarity of air law nor a new development within the field of transportation law. In fact, the long history of maritime transportation law is characterized by an uninterrupted struggle between these two elements. Sometimes the element of lease has been considered the most important, sometimes the element of carriage has dominated.

situation, however, seem to be more closely connected. Even a short glimpse may be enough to reveal that these situations must be "neighbours" in the legal landscape and that the borderline can be expected to be rather vague. In both cases the underlying purpose of the contract is that passengers or goods shall be carried between two points. If one looks to the final main result, the finished transport, the cases are thus perfectly equivalent to each other. But, as regards the performance of the carriage, at least one important difference from a practical point of view is clearly distinguishable: the handling of passengers and goods in case of a sale and purchase of moving space may differ from that in case of a typical transport. This difference can be more or less important, entirely depending on variations in the practical arrangements (loading and unloading, documents used, etc.).

The circumstances now briefly outlined explain why, as stated above, the rules relating to carriage by air sometimes do not function very well when applied to charter agreements. The Warsaw Convention was undoubtedly drafted only with the case of sale and purchase of transportation in mind. To confirm this, it is not necessary to look into the minutes of the Warsaw Conference; the fact is obvious even from a mere examination of the text of the Convention itself and of the construction of its rules. Such an examination is our next task.

In this connection it may be emphasized that the situations now discussed cannot be regarded as examples of successive carriage[2] as they do not concern the distinguishing

[2] As to the interpretation of the concept of carrier in case of successive carriage, see especially *Rotterdamsche Bank N.V. and Banque de l'Indochine* v. *B.O.A.C. and Aden Airways,* (1953) 1 Lloyds List L.R.

of different parts of a transport, each part being performed by a separate carrier. Thus, the situations referred to in this study are not covered by Article 30, which can be left out of consideration.

(2) The difficulties arising when the Warsaw Convention is applied to charter relations are all connected with *the concept of carrier (by air).*

This concept has not been defined in the Convention, though one delegation—the Brazilian one—at the 1929 Conference suggested that the charter problem should be solved by defining the concept in question.[3] But the fact that the Convention lacks an express definition of this kind does not mean that we are left completely without guidance. In some articles it is stated or at least assumed that the carrier may or even must act in one way or another. *It seems to be a reasonable standpoint that on the one hand a person deemed to be a carrier within the meaning of the Convention must also in principle have a practical possibility of acting as described in the same Convention. And, on the other hand, a person satisfying the requirements for a carrier must be subject to the Warsaw Rules—otherwise their character of mandatory rules would have no real effect.* For the moment we will leave open the additional question whether

154; 1953 U.S. & C. Av. R. 163 (High Court of Justice, Queen's Bench Division). Cf. Drion, *op. cit.,* No. 123 (pp. 140—142), and Abraham, *Die internationale Rechtssprechung zum Warschauer Abkommen seit Sommer 1952,* Zeitschrift für Luftrecht 1954, pp. 71 et seq., on pp. 76—77.

[3] See *supra,* Introduction, with references in footnote 2. In 1955, the International Union of Aviation Insurers recommended the same method of solving the problem. See *The Hague Conference, September 1955,* Documentation Vol. 1, p. 128.

or not a person necessarily must be able to act as a Warsaw carrier *in every respect* in order to be treated as a carrier within the meaning of the Convention.[4]

If the principle now presented is accepted as sound, a grouping together of the relevant articles must characterize the carrier by giving an answer to the question of what functions a carrier is supposed to perform. This method can thus be expected to reveal, indirectly, the main points of the concept of carrier on which the Convention is based. The description of the method of interpretation now suggested is certainly a very vague one, as the principle has to be considerably deepened before it is able to show its value. As stated here, the principle can only point to an appropriate direction for further analysis.

An indispensable condition for the correctness of a method of interpretation like the one just suggested is naturally that the term "carrier" is assumed to have the same meaning in the whole Convention. Perhaps someone trying to interpret the Convention might argue that it uses two or more different concepts of carrier. The word "carrier" could, according to this opinion, have a special meaning in Article 22 (concerning the limits of liability) distinct from the meaning of the same word in other articles.[5]

However, such a theory, involving a serious complication of the Convention, is supported neither by the text nor by

[4] This problem is touched upon *infra* (4) and (7).

[5] Drion, *op. cit.*, No. 120 (p. 137), seems to consider this as a possibility ("... both the charterer and the operator would be carrier in the sense of the Convention, at least of Article 22 ..."). Probably he is aiming only at the special case of successive carriage, Articles 1 (3) and 30, as compared with all other provisions about the carrier, cf. No. 118 (p. 134) and *supra*, Ch. III (2).

the discussions when the Convention was drafted. It would, in fact, destroy the functional connection between the various provisions about liability, which together must form a unity. In consequence, it is a highly justifiable supposition that the concept of carrier does not vary from article to article but has a uniform meaning throughout the Convention.

(3) The various *functions of a carrier* within the meaning of the Warsaw Convention may be briefly described as follows.

a. The carrier is *one of the two parties* to the transport agreement, the other being the passenger or shipper. As far as the transportation of goods is concerned this is obvious from the fact that the carrier issues the air consignment note, Articles 5–9, and this document is *prima facie* evidence of the conclusion of the contract, Article 11 (1). Furthermore, the requirement that the points of departure and destination must be determined by the parties in order to constitute a borderline between international carriage and non-Warsaw transports, Article 1 (2), cannot possibly be understood otherwise than as meaning that the carrier is a party to the contract through which this requirement is fulfilled. And according to Article 33, which—like Article 1 (2)—covers transportation of passengers as well as of luggage, it is the carrier who may refuse to enter into any contract of carriage.

b. The carrier *issues passenger tickets, luggage tickets and air consignment notes (air waybills)*, Articles 3 (1), 4 (1), 5 (1) and 6 (3–5). These documents *(the transportation documents)* must contain, among other particulars, the name and address of the carrier or—in the case of successive carriage—carriers (or the first carrier), Articles 3 (1d), 4 (3c) and 8 (e). The most important thing to be observed in this connection is that the carrier is not entitled to avail himself of those provisions which exclude or limit his liability, if he does not issue the required documents or if the luggage ticket or air consignment note does not contain the required particulars, Articles 3 (2), 4 (4), 5 (2) and 9.[6] These particulars are as follows. A luggage ticket must contain the number of the passenger ticket, the number and weight of the package and a statement that the carriage is subject to the rules of the Convention. An air consignment note must contain a great many particulars, of which perhaps the most interesting from our point of view are the nature of the goods, the number of the packages, the method of packing and the particular marks or numbers upon them and, finally, the weight, the quantity, the volume or dimensions of the goods.[7]

c. As to the transportation of goods, the carrier is supposed to have *the possibility of checking the consignor's statements relating to the quantity, volume and condition of the goods*, Article 11 (2). It also may be mentioned that according to Article 10 (2) the carrier can suffer damage by reason of the irregularity, incorrectness or incompleteness of the particulars

[6] A detailed examination of the items required has been made by Drion, *op. cit.*, Nos. 250—273 (pp. 299—314).

[7] The last provision, Article 8 (i), calls for a short comment. The original French text runs as follows: "... le poids, la quantité, le volume ou les dimensions de la marchandise...". The official English translation of this sentence is the following: "... the weight, the quantity *and* the volume or dimensions of the goods..." (my italics). The English version thus requires three particulars but the French text only one statement in the air consignment note on this point. The Warsaw Convention was drawn up in a single text in French only. In consequence, the French version must be regarded as the correct one. Cf. Drion, *op. cit.*, No. 269 (pp. 310—311).

stated by the consignor. However, this fact does not seem to be characteristic of a carrier as such, as many other persons can suffer damage for the same reason, e.g. a passenger, a shipper or a third party.[8] For the concept of damage in the sense of Article 10 includes such different cases as Customs fines imposed because of incorrect description of the goods and damage caused by the goods to aircraft or property of the carrier or of other cargo owners, owing to the fact that the carrier was not informed about the true nature of the goods.[9]

d. According to Article 1 (3), *the carriage is "performed" by the carrier,* cf. Article 30. This expression indicates that the carrier is the executor of the transport, has the direct contact with the passengers in the course of the transport and handles the goods. As regards the transportation of goods, this interpretation is confirmed by other circumstances. The air consignment note is *prima facie* evidence of the receipt of the goods, and consequently the carrier "receives" the goods intended for carriage, Article 11 (1). Furthermore, the carrier has the right to require and is obliged to receive the air consignment note from the consignor, and the second part of the note must accompany the goods, Articles 5 (1) and 6 (2). Documents which are to accompany the air consignment note will be handed over to the carrier, as provided for in Article 8 (o), obviously because the carrier handles the goods. The consignor is liable to the carrier for any damage occasioned by the absence, insufficiency or irregularity of any information or document necessary to comply with Customs, octroi or police formalities

[8] Cf. the text of Article 10 (2): "... all damage suffered by the carrier or any other person ...".

[9] Drion, *op. cit.,* No. 272 (p. 312).

before the goods can be delivered to the consignee, unless the damage is due to the fault of the carrier or his agents, Article 16 (1). And in Article 18 (2) the luggage or goods are said to be "in charge of the carrier" in the course of the transport, irrespective of whether the goods are situated in an aerodrome or on board an aircraft, or, in the case of a landing outside an aerodrome, in any place whatsoever.

e. According to Article 12, the consignor has, up to a certain moment, *the right to dispose of the goods being carried.*[10] He can withdraw them from the aerodrome of departure or destination, or stop them in the course of the journey on any landing, or call for them to be delivered at the place of destination or in the course of the journey to a person other than the consignee named in the air consignment note, or require them to be returned to the aerodrome of departure. All these operations are supposed to be *performed by the carrier,* the consignor having nothing more to do than give his orders, Article 12 (3). This arrangement is understandable only if the carrier executes the transport and handles the goods.

f. The carrier obviously is considered to have *the operational control* of the flight in the sense that he has the possibility of altering the agreed stopping places in case of necessity, Articles 3 (1c) and 8 (c).

g. The carrier is liable for injuries to the passengers and for destruction, loss of or damage to registered luggage and goods, and for damage occasioned by delay, Articles 17–19. This does not necessarily mean, of course, that the carrier

[10] The provisions on this subject may cause some trouble as regards their interpretation, but it does not seem necessary or even appropriate to deal with these problems in this study.

must have the possibility of causing the damage himself—it is one thing to cause damage, another thing to be liable for the damage caused. But, according to Article 20 (1), the carrier is not liable if he proves that he and his agents have taken all necessary measures to avoid the damage or that it was impossible for him or them to take such measures. This provision must be based on the view that the carrier has *the technical control* of the flight in the sense that he really has the practical possibility of taking measures to avoid damage. Otherwise, the duty of the carrier to take such measures would lack any meaning.[11] On the same base rests Article 20 (2), stating that the carrier, as far as the carriage of goods and luggage is concerned, has no liability if he proves that the damage was occasioned only by negligent pilotage or negligence in the handling of the aircraft or in navigation and that, in all other respects, he and his agents have taken all necessary measures to avoid the damage.

h. Articles 18 (1) and 20 (1) reach even further and cover cases, e.g., where the goods have been lost in the course of the transport because of bad organization of the handling procedure or for some other similar reason (commercial faults). The carrier must therefore also have *the commercial control.* This requirement may appear to be a consequence of the fact that the carrier "performs" the transport and handles the goods (*d*).

i. As has now been mentioned (*g–h*), the carrier is allowed

[11] The expression "or that it was impossible for him or them to take such measures" does not mean that the carrier is exculpated if he and his agents have no practical possibility of controlling the technical operations for the reason that someone else has this control. No doubt has ever arisen as to this opinion.

to prove that he and his agents have not been negligent. If he succeeds in proving this, he is free from liability. In order to use this right of exculpation, the carrier naturally *must have access to all materials necessary to prove the non-negligence.*

j. It is the carrier's duty to hand over the air consignment note and to *deliver the goods* to the consignee on arrival of the goods at the place of destination, Article 13.[12]

k. Finally, attention is called to the fact that the carrier is the person to whom *complaints* of damage to baggage and goods must be made according to Article 26.

(4) Bearing all these various functions, typical of a Warsaw carrier, in mind, we are next forced to decide whether they are all equally important or whether one of them, or perhaps several of them, can be considered as more important than the others.

Let us suppose that the idea of prevention is held to be the main rationale of the Warsaw liability rules. It would then be possible to argue as follows: "The technical control (*g*) must always be more important than any other function mentioned. Only a person executing the carriage can be influenced by the liability rules to take precautionary measures. If, for instance, someone else has issued the transportation documents, this fact would not change the result, as the issuance of documents with the required particulars is a mere

[12] The provisions in Articles 12–14, concerning the right to dispose of the goods (*supra* under *e*) and the delivery of the goods at the place of destination, can be varied by express provision in the air consignment note; Article 15 (2). It may be doubted whether the contractual freedom at this point extends very far, but this problem must be left aside in this study.

formality. The person issuing documents cannot influence the execution of the air carriage, but the person having the technical control would perhaps be able, at least in principle, to influence the issuance of the documents, for example by stipulating a fine for breach of the contract between him and the issuing person, if there are no documents issued in their prescribed form. As a consequence, the person executing the carriage must always be the carrier and responsible according to the Warsaw Rules, if the idea of prevention is regarded as decisive."[13]

However, this way of estimating the relative importance of the various carrier's functions cannot, in the author's view, be approved. It is extremely difficult or perhaps even impossible to describe correctly in detail the policy behind the Convention, which of course represents a compromise between many conflicting opinions and interests. Anyhow, it seems unlikely that the idea of prevention was intended to be or could possibly be regarded as the root of the liability. On the contrary, the leading principles behind the Convention are more often stated to be the following, viz. to achieve international uniformity, to guarantee passengers and shippers a minimum compensation in case of damage and to give air carriers the advantage of limited liability. These aims do not necessarily point to the technical execution of the carriage as the most important item. Moreover, the non-appliance of the Warsaw Rules might not always be opposed to the idea of prevention. The opinion that the issuance of the documents in their due form is a mere formality, irrelevant to our problem of interpretation, is indeed con-

[13] Such a standpoint would correspond, as far as the results are concerned, to the one described *supra*, Ch. III (2).

tradicted by the fact that the non-compliance with the requirements of the prescribed documents is sanctioned by loss of the liability limits—and, as has just been pointed out, it is said to be one purpose of the Convention to limit the liability of air carriers.

From these brief remarks it may be gathered that there are good arguments against the sole domination of one point of view and one carrier's function. But it seems self-evident that all the functions mentioned above cannot possess exactly the same weight. Hence, it seems necessary to demonstrate more closely how the author would estimate the relative importance of the various functions typical of a Warsaw carrier. In order to avoid abstract statements, this will be done in connection with the following discussion concerning one example of air charter (7).

(5) We have now briefly described and characterized the relation between the various functions of a carrier as set out in the Warsaw Convention, and at the same time we have in fact sketched the outlines of the concept of carrier within the meaning of the same Convention. On examining the functions mentioned, we shall find that they are all typical of a carrier (e.g. an air transport undertaking) who owns and operates one or more aircraft and "sells transportation" direct to passengers and shippers (concludes contracts of carriage). This must be the typical, the "normal" case, for which the Warsaw Rules are principally intended.[14]

Now the question arises whether it is possible to adapt the rules to charter situations. If the answer is Yes, we must in-

[14] Cf. Drion, *op. cit.*, No. 118 (p. 134).

vestigate how far such an adaptation can be considered adequate.

When trying to solve this problem of interpretation, we must have in mind one practical example of a charter situation, in order to be able to demonstrate the difficulties as clearly as possible. For purposes of convenience the facts of the case here discussed will be simplified—perhaps even oversimplified—by comparison with cases in real life, where there are usually additional circumstances to complicate the picture. These complications will, at least to some extent, be dealt with later on.[15]

Suppose an airplane owner, e.g. an airline company, charters a fully equipped airplane for certain voyages or for a specified period of time to a travel agency or a forwarding agency. The charterer then individually sells the capacity to different passengers and shippers. Here we meet the two main problems already distinguished.[16] Is the Convention applicable to the charter agreement between the airline and the agency? And who is responsible as carrier within the meaning of the Convention in relation to passengers and shippers, the airline or the travel agency?[17] We shall have to examine these two problems separately (6 and 7).

(6) The first question can also be put in this way: does the airline appear *in relation to the travel agency* as a carrier, performing the duties and filling the functions as described in the Convention? To give an answer to this question we

[15] See *infra*, Ch. V.

[16] See *supra*, Ch. II.

[17] For the sake of convenience, the term "travel agency" will here be used as including a forwarding agency, as far as the carriage of goods is concerned.

have to recapitulate the various functions of a Warsaw carrier.

The airline undoubtedly is party to a contract, namely the charter agreement, but according to the given facts it has not entered into any contract with passengers or shippers (*a*). For this reason it cannot in relation to the charterer be said to "perform" any carriage as described above (*d*) or to have any commercial control (*h*). The object of the agreement is not to carry the charterer and his goods but to supply him with moving space, which he can use as he wishes (naturally within the limits agreed with the charterer or provided for in the national law). This implies quite a different procedure as to the handling of the goods and the contact with the passengers. Consequently, the Warsaw Rules seem to be unsuitable.

The airline neither issues the required transportation documents (*b*), nor has it any possibility of checking the consignors' statements relating to the quantity, volume and condition of the goods (*c*). In relation to the charterer the airline cannot act as carrier by exercising the right to dispose of the goods (*e*), as the charterer has no goods of his own on the flights. Furthermore, the airline does not deliver any goods belonging to his contractual party, the agency (*j*), which consequently has no cause to make complaints because of damage to goods (*k*). If not otherwise agreed between the parties, it cannot be assumed that the airline has the right to alter the stopping places agreed with the charterer except for reasons of safety, when a change would probably not be regarded as a breach of contract. Thus, the airline cannot even be said to possess the operational control, as prescribed in the Convention (*f*).

All this seems to be quite clear. On two points, however, there may at first glance appear to be a slight doubt. The airline has of course the technical control of the flight, allowing it to take precautionary measures to avoid damage (*g*), and in addition the airline has access to materials necessary for exculpation (*i*). But these functions do not have exactly the same quality as in the "normal" cases. They are not connected with any duty of the carrier to take care, in the course of the transport, of his contractual party as a passenger or of any goods belonging to or at least shipped by the same party as consignor. There can be no personal injury suffered by the charterer, and the consignor of any goods that may be destroyed or lost is not the same person as the charterer. This situation—the sale and purchase not of transportation but only of moving space—is therefore, in regard to these details also, not in line with the Warsaw pattern of rules concerning the carrier's duties and liabilities.

The conclusion that can be drawn from the facts now stated must be as follows: the Warsaw Convention cannot reasonably apply to the charter contract between the airline and the travel agency.

(7) The second problem seems to be more complicated. Who, *in relation to passengers and shippers,* is responsible as carrier according to the Warsaw Rules—the airline or the agency?

At least one of the two must be deemed responsible as carrier and subject to the mandatory rules of the Convention, since from the passengers' and consignors' point of view there is an ordinary sale and purchase of transportation, i.e. we have exactly the "normal" case covered by the Convention.

Otherwise, it would be very easy to evade the mandatory rules, and so these rules would completely lose their effectiveness. One of the main purposes of making the Warsaw Rules mandatory was to protect the users—passengers and consignors—from wanton dictation and to guarantee a minimum standard of liability for the carrier.

But let us consider the situation from the opposite angle, namely from that of the airline and the travel agency. Is the case from that point of view also in every detail a "normal" one, entirely in harmony with the principles stated in the Convention? The answer to this question must definitely be No. The airline has been in no direct contractual relation to the passengers and consignors. And so far as the travel agency is concerned, this has not executed the carriage.

Here we have found a certain contradiction in the whole problem of interpretation: what from the passengers' and consignors' point of view looks like an ordinary sale of transportation takes on quite a different appearance from the airplane owner's and the charterer's point of view. It seems necessary to recapitulate, once again, the functions of a carrier within the meaning of the Convention in order to investigate how the facts of the case here discussed fit into the Warsaw pattern.

The travel agency has concluded the contracts of carriage with the passengers and consignors (*a*). It has issued the required documents (*b*) and is at the same time in a position to check the consignors' statements relating to the quantity, volume and condition of the goods (*c*). The agency must also be considered to have the operational control as defined above (*f*) and is probably the person to whom complaint should be made (*k*). But here the ability of the travel agency to fulfill the functions of a Warsaw carrier ceases. The agency does not execute the carriage (*d*), cannot perform the consignors' orders as to the disposal of the goods in the course of the transport (*e*), has no technical or commercial control (*g–h*), cannot deliver the goods to the consignees (*j*) and does not have access to all materials necessary for the exculpation (*i*).

This inability is in every respect due to the fact that the travel agency does not itself fulfill its obligation to carry but enlists the help of the airline as a servant, agent or independent contractor. This means that the agency has to rely upon the airline as far as the last-mentioned duties are concerned. It is true that these circumstances may not cause any serious trouble. For, from the agency's point of view, it may make no great difference whether its duty to deliver the goods to the consignees is performed by its own personnel, for whom the agency is liable, or by the airline's personnel, under the condition that the agency has also to be responsible for their performing the said duty. But, on the other hand, there will undoubtedly arise some difficulties that are worthy of consideration.

As for the exculpation, it is obvious that the agency must rely upon the airline to supply it with all necessary proofs concerning precautionary measures. It is not the agency but only the airline that has the direct control over all acts and omissions relating to the performance of the flight. One reason why the carrier, according to the Convention, has to prove his non-negligence is that this rigorous liability is supposed to force the carrier to proceed with the highest degree of care when performing the carriage. As the agency does not perform the carriage itself, this purpose of the rule has no relevance. Another reason why the burden of proof is placed on the carrier instead of the passenger or consignor is undoubtedly that the former can more easily furnish the necessary proofs because of his direct connection with the technical organization and execution of the flight. In the case here discussed, however, the agency does not have this position, and the argument is therefore no longer as convincing as in the "normal" case.

One must admit that these objections to the applicability of the Warsaw Convention are serious. Nevertheless, it seems possible to overcome the difficulties to some extent. In practice it is usually a common interest for both the travel agency (the charterer) and the airline (the airplane owner) to secure all possible proofs of non-negligence. From the owner's point of view an activity of this kind is the safest way to prevent a recourse from the charterer on contractual grounds, even if according to applicable rules the charterer in such a case might have to prove the negligence of the owner. And a factor which may concern a commercial air transport undertaking is that it will wish to show that all possible precautionary measures had been taken, since it must try to keep the confidence of the travelling public, which is the necessary basis for a sound air transport industry. For such reasons the construction of the Warsaw liability as a liability with shifted burden of proof cannot, from a practical point of view, be considered as a *decisive* obstacle to the application of the Warsaw Rules to the case. At any rate, the application of the Rules does not appear to be rendered altogether impossible by reason of their construction, though they are certainly not well adapted to govern a situation like the one here discussed. A good (though perhaps rather cynical) additional argument would be that the excuses are in practice very difficult to prove successfully and for that reason do not play a very important rôle.

So much for the position of the agency. The next step must be to answer the question: What about the position of the airline? Can the airline meet all the requirements of a carrier within the meaning of the Convention?

Once again we must state that the answer cannot be an affirmative one. The position of the airline is just the reverse of that of the agency. The airline executes the carriage and can, in consequence, fulfill all the functions typical of a Warsaw carrier that the agency cannot (*d, e, g–j*). But the airline has concluded no contracts of carriage with the passengers and consignors (*a*), has issued no transportation documents (*b*) and has no possibility of checking the consignors' statements as to the goods (*c*). Furthermore, the airline cannot be considered to have the operational control (*f*) and is probably not the right person to receive complaints from passengers and shippers (*k*).

Even here, most of the difficulties might be overcome in practice with the help of one arrangement or another. On one point, however, there remains a most serious argument for not applying the rules of the Convention. The carrier is, as has already been pointed out, obliged to issue transportation documents with all required particulars, and the breach of this duty is "penalized" through loss of the limits of liability; Articles 3 (2), 4 (4), 5 (2) and 9. Bearing this provision in mind it would, indeed, be quite meaningless to use the Warsaw Rules in cases where the "carrier" has no practical possibility of issuing transportation documents in their required form, thus "penalizing" him beforehand and creating a new system of liability quite different from that of the Warsaw Convention, viz. a fault liability with shifted burden of proof but without any limits—this very result being achieved under the strict assurance that the Warsaw Rules are used!

In the particular case here discussed, the airline has in fact issued no transportation documents. But was there any practical possibility for the airline to issue such documents in their required form and to preserve the limits of liability by such a procedure?

As for the passengers, it would have been enough to have some member of the crew deliver purely formal passenger tickets, printed beforehand and containing no or only a few particulars, at the moment when the passengers were boarding the plane. It cannot be denied, however, that such a delivery of tickets—not as complete as those issued by the travel agency individually to each passenger and specifying his name etc.—has the air of a mere face-saving gesture performed in order to act in literal compliance with rules that are neither intended for nor adapted to a situation like this.

As far as the luggage tickets and air consignment notes are concerned, it seems, under the conditions given in the case here discussed, not only inconvenient but even impossible for the airline to issue documents with all required particulars. The airline does not know the number of every passenger ticket and the number and weight of the packages. Furthermore, it has no knowledge of or power to check the following items: the place of departure and destination of every single parcel; the stopping places agreed between the agency and the consignors; the name and address of every single consignor; the name and address of every consignee; the nature of the goods; the number of the packages, the methods of packing and the particular marks or numbers upon them; the weight, the quantity, the volume or dimensions of the goods. At least, it would be practically impossible for the airline to have every consignor make out a new air consignment note, which could be issued by the airline, without applying a new procedure similar to the previous one applied by the agency and, in consequence, causing a considerable waste of time. And the requirement of a double procedure would undoubtedly meet serious objections even from the consignors and would probably not be accepted.

Looking back at the analysis of our second main problem we may summarize the arguments as follows.

In the case here discussed, the functions that are typical of a Warsaw carrier have in fact been divided between the agency and the airline. In other words, the concept of carrier does not necessarily constitute a single unit.[18] The facts of the case do not fit very well into the Warsaw pattern and for that reason the application of the Warsaw Rules will cause some trouble. In spite of this, it cannot be in harmony with the Convention to leave the situation completely outside the scope of the Rules. On the contrary, either the travel agency (the charterer) or the airline (the airplane owner) has to be deemed responsible according to the mandatory Warsaw Rules in respect of passengers and consignors, as the situation from their point of view appears to be a regular sale and

[18] This is by no means a peculiarity of air law. The same phenomenon can, for instance, be found in maritime law, where the typical functions of the carrier may be divided between the owner of the vessel and the charterer.

purchase of transportation subject to the Convention. Otherwise the mandatory character of the rules would be ignored.

The choice between the agency and the airline as responsible carrier has to be based on an investigation as to which of them is *best situated* to fulfill, under the conditions here specified, the functions of a Warsaw carrier. In our case, the agency was found to have no direct access to the necessary proofs of non-negligence, and the airline was found practically unable to issue all transportation documents in their required form. Of these difficulties, the first was for certain reasons said not to constitute a decisive obstacle to the application of the Convention. It must therefore be of less importance than the second. The practical possibility of issuing transportation documents with all particulars and thus of being able to preserve the limits of liability must be a circumstance of great importance when deciding the applicability of the Convention. And exactly the same can be said from the passenger's or consignor's point of view. To him the person who has, in his own name, issued, or at least should have issued, the transportation documents normally appears as the "real" party of the contract, selling transportation just like any carrier subject to the mandatory Warsaw Rules, and therefore also as the one who must be responsible for any breach of this contract.

For these reasons it seems appropriate to consider the travel agency, as having the status of carrier, liable according to the Warsaw Convention.

This solution of our problem means that the person deemed to be carrier need not be able to fulfill the various functions of a Warsaw carrier in absolutely every respect. The lack of one or perhaps more minor functions may, if necessary, be ignored. Of course, the concept of carrier does not, even according to this method of interpretation, vary from article to article but is the same throughout the Convention: once a person is classified as carrier he is considered to be carrier in all respects and subject to all the rules concerning carriers. But the typical effect of the method here recommended can be described as follows. The concept of carrier has been found to contain a great many characteristics, *a–k*. However, one or perhaps more of these are alternative in the sense that under certain circumstances they can be absent without the classification of the person in question as carrier being changed. To take only one example, the combination of *a–f, h* and *j–k* (*g* and *i* being missing) might in some cases be quite sufficient. The use of this technique of constructing legal concepts may seem a little confusing but is still by no means unknown in other fields of law.

(8) When analyzing the various carrier functions of an airplane owner and a charterer we must take account of the fact that *one of them might act as an agent* for the other, the latter being his principal. He then, as a rule, directly binds his principal. The travel agency in our case will perhaps conclude the contracts of carriage and issue the transportation documents only as a representative of the airline. In such a case the typical carrier functions are in fact not divided between the airline and the agency but are concentrated in the airline, and the difficulties just described will not arise.

In this connection, interest must be focused on a special type of contracts called *interline traffic agreements.* According to the IATA (International Air Transport Association) standard interline traffic agreement each party to the contract is authorized to issue or complete any transportation document and to accept any such document. From the wording of certain clauses it is clear that the issuing airline is to be deemed to act only as an agent of the carrying airline (III:1 and V:1). The issuing airline agrees to pay each carrying airline the transportation charges applicable to the carriage performed by the carrying airline, and these payments are made in accordance with an international system of clearing (VI:1–2). Any airline desiring to become a party to the agreement has to make a written application to the Traffic Director of IATA, and after a certain procedure is observed he may be accepted as a party (IX). The agreement may be executed in any number of counterparts, all of which shall be taken to constitute one original instrument (XI).

As may be clear from these brief remarks, the effect of such an agreement is in fact very similar to that of a multilateral convention. The many airlines that have made the required application and have been accepted as parties are all bound in relation to each other according to the corresponding agreements, and the text of the standard agreement can therefore be said to play the rôle of a binding "convention". A great many airlines are parties to this agreement, and any member of that group of carriers is able to issue transportation documents as agent for any of the other parties.

Is this agreement of any importance when deciding the applicability of the Convention to charter relations?

If Airline A issues a transportation document and in this

mentions Airline B, also a party to the agreement, as carrier, the agreement will have the effect of authorizing Airline A to issue the document on behalf of Airline B, which thus has directly become a party to the contract of carriage concluded. So far there can be no doubt.

But can the existence of the interline traffic agreement influence the results achieved by an interpretation according to the method here recommended?

Suppose that Airline A issues the documents without mentioning any other airline as carrier. However, the carriage is performed by a fully equipped airplane, owned by Airline B and chartered by Airline A. This may be an exceptional arrangement for this particular occasion; or the flight may be regularly flown by Airline B under the same conditions, although Airline A appears, so far as is shown in the transportation documents and time tables, to perform the flight through its own organization. The charter agreement stipulates that Airline B shall keep the transportation charges paid by passengers and consignors.[19]

This would be a case covered by the IATA interline traffic agreement. For it is not required that an airline other than the issuing airline shall be mentioned in the documents as carrier or shall otherwise appear as carrier. On the contrary, the intention has been that the question who will really perform the carriage can remain in abeyance until the very last minute before the actual take-off: the carrier is the airline that actually carried the passengers or goods, and every flown ticket coupon or consignment note is payable within the limits of the agreed clearing procedure. In other words, while the creditor is the passenger or shipper that

[19] This condition can be found in practice in air charter business.

paid the transportation charge, the debtor is until the very last minute in fact not definitely individualized but can be anyone within the group of airlines that are parties to the interline traffic agreement.

This arrangement is of course a very convenient one from the airlines' point of view, and in some cases its flexibility guarantees the customers a faster service. Anyhow, the internal agreement cannot possibly have any other external effect as to persons outside the agreement[20] than to constitute a regular authorization to issue the documents as mentioned before. Otherwise the airline, which issues the transportation documents under its own name and appears to the passengers and consignors as the carrier, would until the very beginning of the carriage easily be able to contract out of the liability according to the mandatory Warsaw Rules, which would be contrary to the rationale of the Convention. Passengers and consignors still have, in principle, freedom to choose whom they want to have as their debtor. The existence of an express provision reserving the right for the carrier to substitute without notice alternate carriers or aircraft[21] cannot possibly be supposed to change this by affecting the liability of the contracting carrier, based upon the mandatory rules.

This seems to be a good reason for excluding the existence of an interline traffic agreement from the circumstances relevant for deciding the applicability of the Warsaw Convention, but with the very important exception that such

[20] Cf. the remarks concerning clauses in charter contracts declaring that one of the parties—either the airplane owner or the charterer—is to be deemed carrier in relation to third parties. See *infra*, Ch. VI.

[21] The IATA General Conditions of Carriage contain such a provision.

an agreement represents one method of authorization, making the issuing airline an agent for the airline set out as carrier in the transportation documents.

(9) What is characteristic of the previously surveyed and criticized methods for deciding the scope of the Warsaw Convention as compared with the method of interpretation here recommended?

From the analysis of different methods of interpretation suggested we have found that, e.g., the requirement of some element of transportation in the agreement, when used alone, gives rise to a certain amount of trouble regarding the extent of the meaning of the term "carriage" ("transportation"). Somewhat the same can be said about the opinion that there must be a direct relation between, on the one hand, the person or undertaking who concluded the contract of carriage and, on the other hand, the passenger or consignor with whom the contract was made. If used alone, this test might indicate that the issuing of required documents, not being necessary for the existence or the validity of the contract of carriage, was unimportant, though this would be contrary to what has been one result of this analysis. The requirement that the charterer can be considered as passenger or consignor within the meaning of the Warsaw Rules seems to be closely connected with the opinion of directness of relationship between the contracting parties and also with the condition that transportation documents shall have been issued or at least that a practical possibility of issuing them should exist.

It is a striking feature that while each of these suggested tests possesses some features which are quite sound, probably none of them, if used alone, is capable of giving satisfactory results. The explanation of this seems to be that every suggested test, however reasonable it may be, only constitutes *one fragment of a more complicated context.* A proper and practicable solution must take account of *all relevant circumstances.*

The border line of relevancy can naturally be drawn in different ways. It has been the aim of this analysis to concentrate on the "Warsaw pattern": *circumstances directly mentioned in or at least appearing as consequences from the Convention itself and the construction of the rules therein.* This method of interpreting the Convention is thus based on the characteristics of the Convention itself. Circumstances which have no reference whatsoever to this—e.g. the question of who has been granted the permit to operate a certain scheduled route and thus has the operational control and liability from the viewpoint of administrative law—have been considered to be of no relevance when solving the problem of interpretation. As may be clear already from the introduction to this study, only a method which uses arguments mainly of "international" character (in other words, arguments derived from the Convention itself) can be expected to promote a solution that has any chance of being accepted by lawyers representing different legal systems.

(10) The investigation of our problems of interpretation has been made with only one uncomplicated example of an air charter situation in mind. The circumstances in other cases may, as has already been pointed out, vary considerably from case to case. Hence, every situation has to be solved from its own characteristic pattern of relevant circumstances.

It is, to take only one example, obvious that the main

obstacle to accepting the airline in the case discussed in this chapter as a responsible carrier within the meaning of the Convention vanishes if the airplane owner has the practical possibility of issuing, and does in fact issue, new transportation documents in their required form before the actual take-off of the plane. In such a case, the issuance of the documents and the access to all materials necessary to prove the non-negligence are linked to the same person, the airplane owner, as soon as he has issued the new documents. The problem may here arise whether the travel agency in our example as the first carrier should then be completely left outside the contract of carriage or if both should be held responsible as carriers side by side; this problem will be discussed later on.[22]

From what has now been said it may be gathered that the actual issuance of, or practical possibility of issuing, the required transportation documents is a circumstance that in many cases is of the utmost importance and certainly influences the results achieved by the method of interpretation here recommended. As to this point, perhaps one major objection could be made, to the effect that such a method of interpretation would mean the attribution of a greater importance to the formalities concerning the transportation documents than these formalities really deserve. The answer to this objection seems to be that the standpoint here taken is inevitable as long as the non-compliance with the requirements of transportation documents is sanctioned by loss of the liability limits. This sanction has been much criticized, and it is easy to understand that the courts have now and then tried to interpret the Convention on this point as

[22] See *infra,* Ch. V (8).

favorably as possible for the carriers.[23] An additional criticism might be that this sanction undoubtedly was not intended to influence the solution of the problem concerning the scope of the Convention.

[23] See for an example the Supreme Court, New York County, in *American Smelting and Refining Co.* v. *Philippine Airlines,* 1954 U.S. & C. Av. R. 221.

Chapter V EXAMINATION OF DIFFERENT TYPES OF SITUATIONS RELATING TO AIR CHARTER

It remains to demonstrate the results to which the solution of our problem of interpretation described in the preceding chapter may lead. This will be done by discussing some practical situations in order to find out where the Warsaw Convention, according to our interpretation, applies. The intention is by no means to cover all the possible combinations of circumstances and arrange the material systematically, but only to pick out some situations that seem practical or otherwise interesting.

(1) An airline charters an aircraft with full operational crew to a person who uses the aircraft for himself or for transportation of his own cargo. The agreement may cover one or more specified journeys (voyage charter) or transportation during a specified period of time (time charter). In this case the airplane owner clearly appears as carrier in relation to the charterer, as long as he has the possibility to fulfill the functions of a Warsaw carrier. The Warsaw Rules definitely apply.[1]

[1] The same opinion is argued by, e.g., Litvine, *op. cit.*, No. 178 (p. 133). See for an example of a charter case of this type *Société Air-Algerie*

The issuance of transportation documents might occasion some slight inconvenience in the case of time charter only, where the charterer first has to decide each journey. However, it cannot be said that this inconvenience usually causes any serious difficulties when applying the Warsaw Rules. But if the aircraft owner would in any case really have no practical possibility of issuing transportation documents, the Convention can no longer apply. Such cases may, however, in practice be very rare, especially as the standard charter agreements often contain provisions according to which the char-

v. *Société Fuller Frères et Société Cotaufruits,* Revue française de droit aérien 1951 p. 433 = Revue générale de l'air 1951 p. 535 (Cour d'appel de Paris, 1re Chambre). In this case, however, the question of the applicability of the Warsaw Convention was never discussed at length, but the Convention was applied for the sole reason that the transportation was an international one and as such governed by the Convention. Cf. Drion, ICAO Doc. 7229-LC/133, p. 133 *in fine:* "... the borderline between ordinary carriage and charter carriage was a very vague one. A shipper who had much business with the carrier might, in order to get a cheaper rate, prefer to have all his shipments carried under charter in one aircraft. For all practical purposes, such carriage should be considered ordinary carriage and there was no reason why the liability of the carrier towards the charterer in these cases should not be governed by the Convention." For another illustration of the close relationship between ordinary carriage and the type of charter carriage here mentioned, see the case referred to by Knauth in Citeja discussions 1936 ("the Clause case") and quoted by Riese, *Die Arbeiten der C.I.T.E.J.A. seit der Berliner Tagung (1934), II,* Archiv für Luftrecht 1937, pp. 40 et seq., on p. 64, footnote 25: "La compagnie avait chaque jour un avion qui vole de Miami à Tampa, soit un vol de quatre heures. Cet avion avait trois ou quatre places. Le jour où M. Clause devait partir, il était seul passager. Il a acheté un billet tout simplement. ... C'est un contrat entre la compagnie et M. Clause. Il était seul passager, mais il y avait encore trois places. On lui demandé: à quelle heure voulez-vous partir? Il a répondu: quelle est l'heure de votre départ? — 9 heures. — C'est un peu tôt... — 9 heures et demie, si vous voulez. On a accepté et à 9 heures et demie il est parti."

terer has to prepare air consignment notes and supply the owner with all documents required.[2]

(2) The situation is exactly the same as the one just described (1), but the charterer also invites his family or some of his friends to join the flight without remuneration, i.e. at the charterer's expense.[3] What is now the relationship (*a*) between the invited persons and the owner of the aircraft and (*b*) between the invited persons and the charterer? If the charterer is the carrier within the meaning of the Convention, the Convention does not apply, as the carriage is gratuitous and not performed by an air transport undertaking; Article 1 (1). But if the owner is deemed to be carrier, the Convention applies, as the owner in the example given is an airline company.

Of course, the solution last mentioned is, from a public point of view, the most desirable one, and it also seems to be the one arrived at by the method of interpretation here suggested. Only the airline company is able to fulfill the various functions of a Warsaw carrier. This is true also as regards the issuance of the tickets and other documents. If no individual tickets have been issued, the airline (the owner of the airplane in the case mentioned), from the invited persons' point of view also, appears to be the carrier and the right person to issue tickets. That it was the charterer who invited them cannot change the picture, as one does not

[2] Cf. *supra,* Ch. III (3), footnote 34.

[3] This was, in fact, the situation in the much-discussed case *Fosbroke-Hobbes* v. *Airwork, Ltd., and British American Air Services, Ltd.,* 1938 U.S. Av. R. 194 (High Court of Justice, King's Bench Division). See *supra,* Ch. III (5). But this case did not raise the question of the applicability of the Warsaw Rules.

expect a private person to issue tickets. If the airline really has issued individual tickets, there will be no doubt that the airline also is the carrier. In both these cases the Warsaw Rules thus apply to the contractual relationship between the invited persons and the airline; that they apply also to the contract between the private person, who chartered the plane, and the airline, has been shown above (1).

This remains the case when the private person who chartered the airplane has himself issued the tickets and in this sense has held himself out as carrier in relation to the invited persons. For the inviter cannot possibly act as a carrier in accordance with the Warsaw pattern: "perform" the carriage, control the flight, have access to the materials necessary to prove non-negligence, etc. He does not even appear to the invited persons as the right person to issue the transportation documents, because of his status as a private person outside the air transportation business, in fact as a passenger acting as host to some guests.

(3) The owner charters his airplane without crew to a person who uses it himself (e.g. "fly-yourself service", flying clubs) or with his own crew. The agreement may concern one or more specified journeys or a certain period of time.

In this case, a bare-hull charter, the owner can never be considered as carrier in relation to the charterer. The bare-hull charter is, in fact, a kind of lease and does not include any transportation elements.[4] As we have seen from the above survey of various methods of interpretation, all authorities seem to be quite unanimous on this point. The finally decid-

[4] Cf. for example Alten, *Deux définitions du terme "exploitant"*, Studi in onore di Antonio Ambrosini, Milano 1955, pp. 31 et seq., on p. 34.

ing argument might be that the agreement is not a contract of carriage but the mere demise of an airplane and that it is practically impossible to apply the Warsaw Rules to a bare-hull charter. In other words, this case definitely does not fit into the Warsaw pattern. The aircraft owner does not "perform" the carriage, he has no control whatsoever over the flight or over the goods in the course of the journey, etc. And it would generally—but not always, see *infra* (5)—be impossible for the owner of the aircraft to issue transportation documents. As an additional argument it may be considered that in all cases of bare-hull charter it would be impossible for the owner to prove, in the strict sense of the word, that he and *his agents ("préposés")* according to Article 20 had taken all necessary precautionary measures, as the crew cannot be qualified as his agents. To apply the Warsaw Rules under such circumstances would in fact mean the construction of a new system of liability, namely a liability founded on an *irrebuttable presumption* of fault.

(4) Airline A, which runs an intercontinental service, has, according to the timetable, its airplanes grounded at a foreign airport of destination for about 30 hours before the departure back to the home airport. The mechanical overhaul of the planes takes only about 10 hours. During the remaining 20 hours the planes are in fact standing idle at the foreign airport. At the same time, there is an increasing demand for air transportation between that airport and an airport in a third country. Airline B of that foreign country, operating regular services on its own routes, therefore charters the non-equipped planes of Airline A while these are idle, in order to operate them with crews belonging to Airline B

on the service mentioned above. This is a case of a so-called *interchange agreement* (interchange of equipment).

The charter contract between Airline A and Airline B is here a kind of bare-hull charter, which for reasons just mentioned (3) cannot be covered by the Warsaw Convention. Airline B, issuing its own tickets, and performing the carriage with its own crew, is here undoubtedly the carrier in relation to the passengers and consignors just as Airline A is the carrier in relation to *its* passengers and consignors. In other words, the passengers and consignors of Airline B have nothing to do with Airline A. Thus, the interchange agreements do not give rise to any particular legal problems.[5]

The same can be said even in respect of the more complicated interchange agreements used for through services.[6] Airline A and Airline B run in pool an international service on a route between the three towns X, Y and Z. The crews of Airline A are used on the flights between X and Y, and the crews of Airline B are used between Y and Z. But for reasons of economy and time-saving the same airplane, belonging to either A or B, is used for the whole journey; only the crews are changed. Airline A issues the transportation documents under its own name, mentioning itself as the *first* carrier. This is clearly a case of successive carriage within the

[5] But in other respects some difficulties may arise. If, for instance, the service of Airline B in the example mentioned in the text was only a domestic one, would it be considered as a breach of cabotage rights (the Chicago Convention Article 7), as *the aircraft,* as a matter of fact, is of foreign nationality (and the foreign airline obviously makes a profit, namely the charter price, out of the domestic service)?

[6] For facts about this type of airline service in the U.S., see Winkelhake, *Interchange Service among the Airlines of the United States,* The Journal of Air Law and Commerce 1955, pp. 1 et seq.

meaning of Article 30 of the Warsaw Convention, which applies to the relationship between, on the one hand, both airlines (the carriers) and, on the other, the passengers or consignors. Each carrier is then deemed to be one of the contracting parties to the contract of carriage insofar as the contract deals with that part of the carriage which is performed under his supervision. The agreement between the two airlines, however, has naturally nothing to do with contracts of carriage and is not covered by the Convention.

If Airline A still issues the transportation documents under its own name, but it is unknown and could not reasonably have been known[7] to the other contracting party that part of the transport is going to be carried out by another carrier, there can no longer be any question of successive carriage. To the passengers and consignors Airline A alone appears to be the carrier.

As far as the part of the carriage performed by the crew of Airline A is concerned, no complications will arise, as this airline company is then practising all the functions of a typical Warsaw carrier. The Convention thus applies to the relationship between, on the one hand, the airline company and, on the other, the passengers and consignors.

But there might be some doubt as to the other part of the carriage, that performed by the crew of Airline B. We are here, in fact, facing a situation that somewhat resembles the one discussed at length above, Ch. IV (7). In many respects Airline A is still acting as a Warsaw carrier. But it can no longer be said to execute the carriage or to perform the consignors' right to dispose of the goods in the course of the transport. It has no technical or commercial control, cannot

[7] Cf. Ch. IV (1), footnote 2.

deliver the goods to the consignees and has no access to all materials necessary for exculpation. All these functions are instead fulfilled by Airline B.

For reasons given above, the practical possibility of issuing the transportation documents with all particulars required to preserve the limits of liability must be a circumstance of great importance when deciding the scope of the Convention. It must be admitted that it would be a most unpractical arrangement to force Airline B to make out new sets of tickets and consignment notes when taking over the performance of the carriage. Such an arrangement having the sole aim of preserving the limitation of responsibility, would mean an intolerable waste of time, money and energy. Therefore, Airline A seems, under the given circumstances, to be the one best situated to fulfill the most important functions of a Warsaw carrier and thus to be responsible as such. Airline B will then be regarded as an agent or an independent contractor.

As some doubt can obviously arise in situations of this type, it is always advisable to arrange transportation carried out under an interchange agreement on the basis of successive carriage, thus escaping all difficulties as to the applicability of the Convention in relation to passengers and consignors.

(5) A big airline finds that it cannot cut down costs sufficiently to operate a short feeder line on a sound economic basis. A small air charter company, however, with no large and expensive organization to support, might possibly be able to work the route on a paying basis. Therefore, the big airline company charters one of its airplanes without crew to the small charter company, which operates the plane with

its own personnel. Nevertheless the airline company still issues the tickets and the consignment notes under its own name.[8] A charter agreement of this type means in fact that the owner at the same time charters back his own airplane, equipped with the crew of the first charterer. This complicated construction of the agreement is responsible for some peculiarities.

The situation is, indeed, quite an extraordinary one. From what has already been said (3), it is clear that the charter agreement (as to the bare-hull charter of the airplane) between the two airline companies falls outside the scope of the Warsaw Rules as not being a contract of carriage within the meaning of the Warsaw Convention. But who is the carrier *in relation to passengers and consignors?*

It is often said that in the case of a bare-hull charter the charterer must, at least generally, be considered as the carrier.[9] He is operating the aircraft with his own personnel. But in the case now mentioned the charterer, who chartered the plane of the airline and supplied the crew, cannot, in spite of the fact that the airline is in reality not much more than a ticket agent of the charter company, be said to appear to the passengers and the consignors as the carrier, their contractual partner. The tickets are still issued by the owner of the airplane. It may be added that the airplane itself bears the inscriptions and trade marks of the owner. The only difference from the passengers' and the consignors' point of view is that the crew wear different uniforms from the

[8] See for an example agreements of March 10 and September 9, 1953, between *Kommanditbolaget M. Ahrenberg* and *SAS.*

[9] Cf. Shawcross & Beaumont, *op. cit.,* No. 513 (C).

personnel of the owner—a very slight and unimportant difference.

To find the solution of this case we have to find out who is really exercising the rights and duties of a Warsaw carrier.

The big airline is undoubtedly contracting partner in relation to passengers and consignors and issues the transportation documents required. It also manages a substantial part of the handling of passengers and goods: it has the possibility of checking the consignors' statements as to the quantity, volume and condition of the goods, it can perform the consignors' right to dispose of the goods as long as these are on the ground, it has the operational control as well as part of the commercial control and the possibility of delivering the goods to the consignees. Furthermore, it seems appropriate to direct complaints arising out of damage to baggage and goods to the big airline company.

What functions typical of a Warsaw carrier are left to the small charter company in these circumstances? This company undoubtedly performs the air carriage and has thus the technical control over the flight as well as access to all materials necessary to prove non-negligence. It can perform the consignors' right to dispose of the goods only when carrying the goods on board the plane. The goods must be delivered to the representatives of the big airline and not directly to the consignees. It is a striking feature that on every point where the small airline company is acting in accordance with the Convention this company *appears* to act rather than really does act as a Warsaw carrier. This is due to the fact that the actions of the small airline company are, to a considerable extent, dependent on the wishes and instructions of the big one. The status of the charter company very much resembles that of an agent helping his principal to carry out his obligation.

Taking into account this entire situation, it seems appropriate to hold the big airline, which chartered its own plane, responsible as carrier within the meaning of the Warsaw Convention in relation to passengers and consignors. This result has the advantage of corresponding with the probable impression of the public, as has already been pointed out. If the solution now given is correct, we are here facing an exception from the rule that in a case of bare-hull charter the charterer is the carrier in relation to passengers and consignors.

(6) A travel agency (including a forwarding agency) charters an airplane with crew for one or more determined voyages or for a specified period of time. The agency then sells the capacity of the plane to individual passengers and consignors, just as an airline would do, and it also issues all transportation documents under its own name. Or a number of small shipments are consolidated by the charterer, who has himself issued, under his own name, separate consignment notes to all the shippers ("consolidated shipments"). This is a brief description of the same situation as that analyzed above, Ch. IV (6–7), in order to illustrate the method of interpretation here recommended. The final result achieved was that the agency in such cases has to be deemed responsible as carrier according to the Convention. The airplane owner can be sued on a Warsaw basis neither by the passengers and consignors nor by the agency.

This solution seems, it may here be noted, to be quite in line with the impression that the users can be expected to get. This is a point which, at least according to Scandinavian law, would be considered of great importance. The travel agency has certainly not done much more than a ticket agent of the airline company would do. But if the situation is regarded from the passengers' and consignors' point of view, it is nevertheless the travel agency which has been held out to the public as the carrier. The contracts of carriage are concluded between, on the one hand, the passengers and consignors and, on the other, the agency as a carrier. Whether the agency itself owns and operates the airplane in question or uses another undertaking's airplane and crew may be an irrelevant circumstance for many persons using the air service. There is no direct contractual relationship between the owner of the airplane and the passengers/consignors.[10]

(7) The situation is exactly the same as that described above (6), with the exception that the travel agency issues the tickets and consignment notes on behalf of the owner of the chartered airplane (usually an airline company). In such a case the travel agency cannot, even from the passengers' and consignors' point of view, be looked upon as more than a ticket agent. The owner of the airplane performs in every respect the rights and duties of a Warsaw

[10] Cf. Saint-Alary, *Le droit aérien* (Collection Armand Colin No. 299), Paris 1955, pp. 152–153: "... il se peut même qu'une agence de voyages traite en son nom avec la clientèle, mais, si cette agence veut décliner ultérieurement toute responsabilité, elle fera bien de ne créer dans l'esprit de la clientèle aucune confusion entre elle-même et l'entreprise de transports, sinon les tribuneaux pourraient bien la considérer comme le transporteur lui-même." An interesting case concerning the application of the Warsaw Rules to contract between shipper and his forwarding agent is *Société "La Neuchâteloise"* v. *Société Aéro-Cargo et al.*, Revue française de droit aérien 1951 p. 440 (Cour d'appel de Lyon, 1re Chambre).

carrier. No difficulty of the kind here described will arise, as the typical carrier functions have in fact not been divided between two persons.

Someone may perhaps ask what purpose is served by the charter agreement between the travel agency and the carrier, as a direct contractual relationship has been established between the owner and every passenger/consignor. The answer to this is chiefly to be found in the matter of remuneration. The agency has chartered the plane for a certain price, and whether the plane's full capacity is used or not is a matter which concerns only the agency, not the owner, who has sold the complete space. A charter contract of this type is, in other words, a monetary agreement. Other particulars, special to the charter agreement, can also give this contract between the owner and the charterer an independence in respect of the contract of carriage.

(8) The situation is still the same as that mentioned above (6). The transportation documents are thus issued by the travel agency under its own name. But just before the departure the owner of the chartered aircraft or his representative issues other transportation documents to each passenger or consignor. What legal effect will such an arrangement have? Is it still the agency that is the carrier within the meaning of the Warsaw Convention? Or is it perhaps that, owing to the new documents, the owner of the chartered aircraft is the carrier? Or are both of them to be considered as carriers at the same time?

The last-mentioned view has sometimes been argued.[11] The

[11] Shawcross & Beaumont, *op. cit.*, No. 362 note (a). Cf. Beaumont, ICAO Doc. 7229-LC/133, p. 133, and McNair, *The Law of the Air*, 2nd

result would be that the Convention would apply to both contracts (but apparently not to the agreement between the owner and the charterer) and the passengers and consignors would be able to sue both the owner and the charterer on a Warsaw basis. It is not expressly stated that the person suffering damage in this case would or would not be able to claim a liability sum up to double limits, if he has not had his damage fully compensated.

The principle of joint liability has been stated in the discussions about the revision of the Warsaw Convention to be desirable *de lege ferenda*. The official IATA point of view has been that all parties to the air charter for transport purposes—owner, operator, lessee or charterer—should be deemed to be carriers and should be jointly and severally liable under the Convention.[12] In the provisional draft prepared by Beaumont in 1951 there was incorporated an article which made the charterer and the operator of the aircraft jointly and severally liable,[13] and a similar standpoint was argued in a Report of 1955 concerning provision relating to charter and hire of aircraft, suggested for inclusion in the Warsaw Convention.[14]

ed. by Kerr & MacCrindle, London 1953, pp. 278–279. Drion, *op. cit.*, No. 120 (p. 137) seems to adopt the idea of two carriers at the same time, if both have concluded contracts of carriage, but is otherwise hesitant, No. 118 (pp. 134–135 with footnote 7).

[12] See Cooper, ICAO Doc. 7229-LC/133, p. 127 *in fine*, 222. Cf. Gazdik, *Analysis of Certain Aspects of the Law of Contracts to International Carriage of Goods by Air* [unpublished manuscript], (Institute of International Air Law, McGill University), Montreal [1950], p. 53.

[13] ICAO Doc. 7229-LC/133, p. 204; cf. *ibid.*, p. 298.

[14] The Hague Conference (September 1955), Doc. 42. The following text was proposed: "Subject to the provisions of Article 30, when the air carriage is performed by a person other than the one in whose name

The problem about the legal effect of the double issuance of tickets can be solved only by judicial interpretation, based on the general rules of the system of national law concerned. In this connection it may be asked why the passengers or consignors should have the improved security of two (or more) responsible persons instead of one, just because of the existence of a charter contract. Are there really any special reasons for this arrangement to be found in those situations? One reason might be that the agency, after having concluded contracts of carriage with passengers and shippers, should not be allowed to place itself entirely outside the mandatory rules of the Warsaw Convention only by having the airplane owner issue a new set of documents. But in many respects it would seem more appropriate to look upon the double issue of transportation documents as a change of the responsible carrier; by issuing new documents the aircraft owner steps into the shoes of the first carrier.

the agreement to carry was concluded, each of such persons shall be jointly and severally liable as a carrier in accordance with the provisions of this Convention. Nevertheless, if only one of such persons is liable under Article 25, the excess above the limits comprised in Article 22 shall be recoverable only from that person." The Norwegian delegation suggested a modified article, Doc. 86, 13/9/55: "*1.* By charter is meant a contract of carriage comprising the whole capacity of an aircraft and concluded either for a specific voyage or a series of voyages (voyage charter) or for a specific time (time charter). 2. When the charterer enters into sub-contracts of carriage, the parties to the charter (operator and charterer) shall be liable jointly and severally to passengers and consignors or owners of cargo. In so far, however, as the internal relations of the parties to the charter are concerned, the provisions of paragraph (1) of article 23 shall not prevent them from agreeing on exoneration clauses." Cf. *The Hague Conference, September 1955,* Documentation Vol. 1, p. 118 (United Kingdom). The result as to this point of the discussions at The Hague was only a Recommendation in the Final Act. See *infra,* Conclusion.

One argument against adopting the system of double carriers might be derived from the particular method of interpretation adopted in this study. As soon as the required documents have been issued by the owner of the aircraft, he has in fact put himself into a new position: he is now in every respect fulfilling or at least able to fulfill the typical functions of a Warsaw carrier. As distinguished from the situation just before the issuance of the documents, he has entered into a direct contractual relationship with passengers and shippers and has at the same time preserved the Warsaw limits of liability. The travel agency has never had and can never acquire such a position, though it once exercised an important part of the rights and duties of a Warsaw carrier and *before* the owner's issuance of new documents was to be deemed responsible as carrier according to the Warsaw Rules (6). As one, and only one, of the persons in question now *completely* meets the requirements of a carrier in the sense of the Convention, the simplest solution must be to qualify him alone, and no one else, as responsible carrier.

(9) In airline practice it is very common for organizations like the Red Cross to charter airplanes for the transport of groups of persons (executives, employees, etc.) or a certain quantity of goods. Such cases are, of course, not different from that of the travel agency (6–8) and must therefore be handled in the same way. The same result is obtained in cases where the airplane owner has chartered a plane to an agent who uses it for a sort of "tramp traffic", i.e. for selling space to a number of merchants for the carriage of cargo between a number of different places.[15]

[15] Cf. Beaumont, ICAO Doc. 6014, LC/111, 16/8/48, p. 123 *in fine.*

A *combination* of different types of charter agreements is not uncommon in practice. "There may be an owner who hires an aircraft (without crew) to an operator who provides the crew and charters the aircraft to a charterer who makes the whole or part of the passenger or cargo accommodation available to one or more agents for specified voyages or for unspecified voyages during a period, and the agents may sell the passenger and cargo space to a number of different persons for different voyages."[16] Instances like this do not, however, give rise to any additional difficulties. The travel agency or the first charterer appears as the carrier from the passengers' or consignors' point of view, and has the best practical possibility of exercising the rights and duties of a Warsaw carrier, as demonstrated above (6–8); only in either of these contractual relationships do the Warsaw Rules apply. The first charter agreement can, as a bare-hull charter, never be covered by the Convention (3). Nor does the charter agreement between the travel agency and the operator fall within the scope of the Convention (6–8).

(10) An airline finds it inconvenient, e.g. for political reasons, to run a certain service to a foreign country under its own name. To overcome this difficulty, it charters planes, whether equipped or not, to an airline company of the foreign nationality, this airline perhaps being controlled by the first company.[17]

If the charter agreement is of the bare-hull type, only the

[16] Beaumont, *ibid.*, p. 124.

[17] An example from the early thirties is given by Slotemaker, *Freedom of Passage for International Air Services*, Leiden 1932, p. 45 *(Imperial Airways* and *Indian State Airway).*

foreign airline company can perform the rights and duties of a Warsaw carrier in relation to passengers and consignors. It not only concludes the contracts of carriage and issues the documents but also operates the service itself. The Convention does not require that the carrier must also be the owner of the plane. As to the agreement between the aircraft owner and the bare-hull charterer, it has already been shown that the Convention never applies (3).

If, however, the agreement provides for the charter of an aircraft with licensed crew, the picture changes in many respects. It is true that the charter agreement still falls outside the scope of the Warsaw Convention. But the problem concerning the applicability of the Convention to the contract between the passengers or consignors and either of the two airline companies becomes more difficult to decide. Again we meet a case where the typical functions of a Warsaw carrier have been divided between two parties. The situation resembles the previously discussed cases (5) and (6–8). In fact, the foreign airline can be said to play the rôle of a travel agency representing the other airline. But in accordance with the purpose of the whole arrangement all transportation documents have to be issued by the foreign airline under its own name. Thus, only the arguments used when discussing case (6) seem to be applicable in this case. In other words, the foreign airline company is believed to be responsible as carrier within the meaning of the Warsaw Convention.

(11) A person has chartered a fully equipped aircraft from an airline on a voyage or a time basis to carry his own merchandise. However, he cannot use the whole capacity of

the plane but needs only two-thirds of the available space. He therefore charters the remaining one-third to another person, who wants to send his cargo to the same place.

In such a case there are two kinds of contracts, the one being an ordinary charter agreement concluded between the owner of the airplane and the charterer, the other being a *sub-charter* contract concluded between the charterer of the plane and the sub-charterer.

From what has been stated before it may be clear that in the circumstances now described the first contractual relation, the charter agreement, is covered by the Warsaw Rules, as long as the goods carried are the charterer's own merchandise (1). But what about the second contractual relation, the sub-charter contract?

In this case also the carrier functions have been divided between two parties. The airplane owner executes the transport but only the charterer has concluded any contract of carriage with the shipper of the goods. Supposing the charterer has issued the documents under his own name or at least had the best practical possibility to issue such documents, he seems to be in the same position as the travel agency under the given circumstances (6) and thus to meet to a decisive extent the necessary requirements for a Warsaw carrier. As the sub-charter contract concerns the transportation of the sub-charterers' own merchandise, this contract is obviously one of the kind to which the Warsaw Rules apply (1).

All contractual relations in which the one party is deemed to be the carrier within the sense of the Warsaw Rules are covered by the Convention. In consequence, there can be two different carriers on one and the same flight: the owner in relation to the charterer and the latter in relation to the sub-charterer. This result is by no means a challenge to the correctness of the solution. That there are two different carriers on the same flight means nothing more remarkable than that we may have to apply two different sets of rules on the same flight, the international rules (the Warsaw Convention) and the national ones, depending on the place of destination mentioned in the transportation documents.[18]

If the charterer has concluded the contract with the sub-charterer on behalf of the aircraft owner, he is clearly acting only as an agent. The owner is then exercising all rights and duties of a Warsaw carrier and is thus responsible as such (7). As to the case where the charterer originally contracted under his own name, but the owner issued new sets of transportation documents before the actual take-off, the same arguments apply as above in case (8).

(12) Special problems may arise in the "*mixed crew cases*". The owner charters—on a voyage or time charter basis—his plane, equipped with only pilots, a flight engineer and a radio operator. The charterer, who perhaps is a travel agency, supplies a purser and a stewardess. The tickets are issued by the owner through the charterer as agent for the owner. During the journey the stewardess, whether negligently or not, spills some very hot coffee on the hands of a passenger, who suffers injury. In consequence of what has been said before, the owner of the airplane appears as the carrier in relation to the passenger. But is the owner of the plane also responsible for those crew-members who are not his employees? The answer to this question apparently depends on

[18] Cf. *supra,* Ch. III (3), at footnote 30.

the interpretation of the term "agent" in Article 20 of the Warsaw Convention (the original French term is "*préposé*"). If the stewardess were deemed not to be an agent of the carrier, the carrier would be inable to excuse himself by proving, in accordance with Article 20, that he and his agents had taken all necessary measures to avoid the damage. Consequently, the acceptance of a carrier's liability for acts of the stewardess would indeed create a new system of liability, contrary to the Convention, namely that of an irrebuttable presumption of fault.[19] However, it may be possible to interpret the word "agent" so widely as to include all persons used by the carrier for the execution of the carriage, e.g. in the example given even the stewardess.[20] In fact, this seems to be the most reasonable interpretation, and it seems to be supported also by the common interpretation of the corresponding term "servant" ("*préposé*") in international maritime law. If this interpretation is accepted, there is no obstacle to making the carrier responsible. It may perhaps also be said that, from the passenger's point of view, the stewardess is "employed" by the owner-carrier in just the same way as in the case of the charter of a fully equipped plane where the owner's personnel are "employed" by the charterer-carrier.

[19] Cf. *supra* (3) *in fine.*

[20] Cf. Goedhuis, *National Airlegislations,* pp. 223 et seq.; Riese, *Luftrecht,* p. 454; Drion, *op. cit.,* No. 196 (p. 238).

Chapter VI WARSAW CLAUSES IN AIR CHARTER AGREEMENTS

All that has now been said about the applicability of the Warsaw Convention to contracts between airplane owners and charterers has been founded on the implied assumption that the parties have not by agreement extended the scope of the Convention. But, as has already been pointed out,[1] it is not uncommon that the owner and the charterer agree that the Warsaw Rules shall apply to a contract which would not automatically have been governed by them.

There are many reasons why the parties may wish to include such a Warsaw Clause in their agreement. The aircraft owner is sure of having his liability limited in a way that can be approved by the courts, instead of risking an order to pay compensation to a higher amount. Insofar as the Warsaw Rules guarantee the charterer a better position than the rules otherwise applicable (the national laws or the special provisions agreed by the parties), an air transport undertaking may find it sound policy to treat all customers in the same way, passengers and consignors as well as charterers. As to the charterer, he might normally consider it an

[1] See *supra*, Ch. II, *in fine*.

advantage to be protected by the mandatory rules of the Convention against wanton dictation by the carrier.

Warsaw Clauses exist in many different wordings. The effect of such clauses must, within the limits of the principle of contractual freedom, be that the parties have by agreement extended the scope of the Convention. This means, of course, that the aircraft owner agrees to exercise all the rights and duties of a Warsaw carrier. One consequence may be obvious from the above analysis. The simple formula that the carriage executed under the charter contract is subject to the rules of the Warsaw Convention may in some cases be dangerous to the owner, as he must then issue the required transportation documents in order to keep his right to avail himself of those provisions which exclude or limit his liability. If he has no possibility or no intention of issuing the documents, this condition would make him liable under the Convention, but without any limits—for him an unexpected result of the clause. To avoid this result, it seems necessary to declare the Convention applicable with the express exception of Articles 3, 4 and 9.[2]

The excluding of some rules in order to adopt only the remaining rules of the Convention is, of course, valid under the principle of contractual freedom. But the national law is likely to require that the intended exceptions be stated

[2] Cf. the preliminary model air charter agreement, drafted by IATA in the spring of 1954, para. 29: "*Carriage* under this Agreement is subject to *the rules relating to liability* established by the Convention for the Unification of Certain Rules Relating to International Carriage by Air signed at Warsaw, October 12th, 1929 (hereinafter called 'the Convention') unless such carriage is not 'international carriage' as defined by the Convention." (Italics added.) The same formula can be found in the draft model air charter agreement, discussed by the Legal Committee of IATA in October 1955.

with accuracy and distinctness. The formula just mentioned —a *paramount clause* containing a reference both to the Warsaw Convention and to the exceptions agreed—would probably be considered to meet those requirements. However, some difficulties as regards this point may arise in cases where the Warsaw Clause has the character of a paramount clause without any exceptions stated therein but where in spite of that some special conditions incorporated in the agreement are contrary to the rules of the Warsaw Convention. To mention one example only, the Swedish Supreme Court has in a case of this type declared as null and void certain exclusions of liability contained in a bill of lading that was used for a transport falling outside the scope of the Hague Rules.[3] The main argument for this interpretation of the document was that this would otherwise appear as intolerably misleading as to the real bearing of the introductory paramount clause, according to which the Hague Rules were to apply to the agreement. The paramount clause was, according to the Court, of basic importance for the agreement and it gave the bill of lading its character. The court also pointed out, as an additional argument, that the exclusions from the carrier's liability provided for in the bill of lading obviously went further than the applicable Swedish law could possibly be expected to approve.

In some standard air charter agreements it is easy to trace the intense efforts made to carry through very thoroughly, in all its details, the principle that the aircraft owner shall be carrier in the exact sense of this concept in the Convention.

[3] *Compagnie Beurrière et Fromagères* v. *Stockholms rederiaktiebolag Svea,* 1951 Nytt juridiskt arkiv avd. I 138.

A typical example is offered by the *KLM Royal Dutch Airlines Aircraft Charter Agreement.*

The carriage is there declared to be subject to certain provisions of the KLM's General Conditions of Carriage, and *the charterer declares that the KLM or its servants or its agents shall not be subject to any higher liability than that provided for* in the said Conditions, or *in the Warsaw Convention* (insofar as this is applicable to the subject transportation), towards any sub-contractor, passenger, shipper or any person having an interest in the carriage or in the persons or goods carried (Article 12). Furthermore, the charterer is not allowed to sub-contract or give in use wholly or in part the chartered space and/or payload of the aircraft without the prior *written approval* of the KLM; unless expressly agreed otherwise in writing, any such approval is given subject to the condition that the sub-contractor shall abide with all obligations imposed upon the charterer and that the charterer shall assume full responsibility for all acts or omissions of the sub-contractor and his servants or agents (Article 9). The charterer agrees to abide by the currently effective Resolutions of the IATA restricting the resale of chartered space (Article 10). As regards the transportation documents, *the charterer undertakes to co-operate in ensuring that* for all passengers, baggage and goods transported pursuant to the agreement *transportation documents are made out* in accordance with the requirements, practices and procedures of the KLM; the charterer promises to provide the KLM with *all information* in connection with passengers, baggage and goods within the time needed for the completion of the documents, and in all these documents *the KLM shall appear as carrier* (Article 13). Finally, the agreement is stated to have been made by the charterer both in his own name and for his own account *and in the names and for the accounts of sub-contractors, passengers, and owners and other parties* having or claiming any interest in the baggage and goods transported pursuant to the agreement (Article 18).[4]

The author of this standard agreement has obviously taken great pains to prevent, in every possible way, any claims being made against the airline company other than those based exclusively on the Warsaw Rules.

The tendency nowadays is, undoubtedly, to have an agreement that the Warsaw Rules shall cover all charter operations with the exception of pure bare-hull charter. The IATA General Conditions of Carriage 1953, which are to a certain extent based on the Convention, declare in Article 2 (3) that, if there are no special charter conditions, a charter carriage performed by a IATA company is subject to the General Conditions.[5] This can be true, however, only insofar as these are not opposed to the mandatory Warsaw Rules, if the Convention applies.

As we have now seen, the aircraft owner and the charterer have, within the limits of the principle of contractual freedom, power to extend the scope of the Warsaw Convention as far as their own contractual relationship is concerned. It

[4] A condition for the validity of this last clause must be that the applicable national law permits an agent to represent persons who, at the time of the contract being concluded, are completely unknown even to himself as regards both number and identity. The IATA draft model air charter agreement 1955 contains a similar clause (para. 15).

[5] Cf. Schweickhardt, *Die neuen Beförderungsbedingungen der IATA für den Luft-Personen- und Gepäckverkehr,* Beiträge zum internationalen Luftrecht (Festschrift für Alex Meyer, Verkehrswissenschaftliche Veröffentlichungen Heft 32), Düsseldorf 1954, pp. 117 et seq., on p. 122.

remains to raise the question whether they can also decide by agreement which of them shall be deemed to be carrier *in relation to passengers and consignors.* If the answer is Yes, the Warsaw Rules would apply to that one of the parties in the charter agreement which is expressly declared to be the carrier within the meaning of the Convention.[6] And this would, in fact, mean that the owner and the charterer would both be free to decide which of them should be the person liable under the Warsaw Rules, i.e. the contract on that subject is intended to have effect against third parties (passengers and consignors).

Naturally it is quite impossible in this short study to sketch even the outlines of the difficult and far-reaching question which immediately arises of the extent to which contracts have effect against persons other than the contracting parties. It may merely be remarked that the usual opinion in common law countries is very much against the recognition of such effects. As regards Continental law, such effects are nowadays recognized more or less willingly in some cases, but as a rule only insofar as they result in a benefit to the third party. The following declaration in the Code Civil, Article 1165, is typical: *"Les conventions n'ont d'effet qu'entre les parties contractantes . . ."*

Already it may be clear from these short remarks that here at least we are facing an important difficulty. Under the common law it may be doubted whether an agreement of

[6] This opinion has been argued *de lege ferenda* by Beaumont in discussions about the revision of the Warsaw Convention. Cf. the debate reported in *Dixième Congrès International de Législation Aérien du Comité Juridique International de l'Aviation (1948),* Paris 1949, pp. 209—219. Critical as to the validity of such clauses is Hesse, *op. cit.,* pp. 64—65.

this kind has any legal effect at all. And under many civil law systems the agreement will be considered as invalid—if not completely irrelevant—in all cases where the third party would have a worse position. If, according to the national legislation or practice, the injured third party has to prove negligence on the part of the tortfeasor in order to get compensation, he must generally be said to have actually been in a worse position than under the Warsaw Convention with its shifted burden of proof, though the liability according to the national rules may be unlimited.

As regards cases automatically governed by the Convention, the problem here discussed seems easy to decide. For it would be contrary to the mandatory character of the Warsaw Rules to allow one of the parties to contract out of his Warsaw liability.

CONCLUSION

On looking back and summarizing the results obtained above, we shall find—if the principles here followed are accepted as sound—that *the Warsaw Rules apply in only a few cases to the contract between the airplane owner and the charterer.* Time and voyage charters fall within the scope of the Convention if the charterer uses the airplane for transportation of himself or of his own merchandise (except for the very rare situation that arises when the aircraft owner really has no practical possibility of issuing the documents required), and also if the family or some friends of the charterer are carried at the invitation of the charterer and at his expense. In other cases the Warsaw Rules do not apply. As to bare-hull charter, the Convention can never cover any kind of such charter agreements. It is a remarkable feature that the line of distinction does not run between time and voyage charter agreements, a fact which confirms that it is unsuitable to base the air charter rules on maritime law concepts.[1]

It has been pointed out above that the concept of charter as used in the air transport industry is a very vague one.[2] As

[1] Cf. *supra,* Ch. I.
[2] *Supra, ibid.*

it seems desirable to bring under a single concept all situations that are governed by approximately the same rules, the term "charter" could with great advantage be limited to the charter agreements outside the mandatory rules of the Warsaw Convention, i.e. all bare-hull charters and time and voyage charters other than the types just mentioned. Within this field, ruled by the principle of contractual freedom insofar as the applicable national law is not opposed to this, it would then be practical to distinguish between charter of non-equipped airplanes (bare-hull charter) and charter of equipped airplanes (irrespective of whether this contract was made on a time or a voyage basis).[3] Perhaps such a limitation of the term "charter" would not, in spite of its theoretical clearness, be approved in practice, since people have already got accustomed to the broader sense of the term. If this terminology cannot be changed, it might at least be possible to introduce one minor improvement: a frequent use of the terms "Warsaw charter" and "non-Warsaw charter" in order to indicate more exactly the type of carriage referred to.

In relation to the passengers and consignors, either the owner or the charterer must be deemed responsible as carrier within the meaning of the Warsaw Convention, which is thus applicable. Consequently, the carrier is now and then a person or undertaking that does not directly engage in air transportation by the operation of the aircraft. It is, by the way, not unusual that (e.g. according to American law) a "common carrier" is a person or undertaking other than the one that actually undertakes the carriage. *One* essential characteristic of this concept is, however, that the carrier shall

[3] For further details, see the article by Grönfors referred to *supra*, Ch. I, footnote 1.

issue a bill of lading or a similar document,[4] i.e. one of the circumstances here found to be important. A disadvantage of this interpretation might be that it would make it possible for an operator to set up a separate carrier company or travelling agency without having sufficient assets, perhaps even being insolvent, and have this latter undertaking issue the transportation documents and fulfill as much of the typical functions of a Warsaw carrier as to be deemed to be the carrier in relation to passengers and consignors.[5] This would, in fact, mean that the operator had placed himself outside the scope of the Convention, in spite of Article 23. If the arrangement was made only to escape liability, it might nevertheless be possible to overcome this difficulty and hold the operator liable as carrier on the grounds that the carrier company or travel agency was only a "man of straw" or that the operator was an undisclosed principal, or on the basis of other rules to the same effect that the national law may contain.[6]

Between the non-carrier—he may be the owner or the charterer—and the passenger or consignor, there is usually no contractual relation. The question of the applicability of the Warsaw Rules therefore never arises. An exception is constituted by the case in which both the charterer and the

[4] Cf. Westwood & Elpern, *Legal Aspects of Air-Carrier Relationships in the Field of Cargo Transportation,* [mimeograph] New York 1944, pp. 195—197.

[5] Cf. Goedhuis, *National Airlegislations,* p. 137; van Houtte, *op. cit.,* No. 77 (p. 123); Shawcross & Beaumont, *op. cit.,* No. 513 note (h); Beaumont, ICAO Doc. 7229-LC/133, p. 204 note 28 (a); Hesse, *op. cit.,* pp. 23, 61—62; Hughes, *op. cit.,* p. 23; Litvine, *op. cit.,* No. 180 *in fine* (p. 135).

[6] Cf. Goodfellow, ICAO Doc. 7229-LC/133, p. 128.

owner issue, each in his own name, the transportation documents, if both persons are then recognized as carriers within the meaning of the Convention.[7]

Finally, a few words may be added about the revision of the Warsaw Convention and its influence on the problem of the applicability of the Warsaw Rules to air charter relations.

At the Hague Conference of September 1955, a Protocol to amend the Warsaw Convention was signed. This Protocol contains important modifications of the Convention but is still based on the old, world-wide system of liability for international air carriage. Particularly important is the simplification as to the formalities required when issuing the transportation documents. The carrier will lose his liability limits only if no passenger ticket or baggage check has been delivered (no air waybill has been made out) or if the document does not include a notice that the Warsaw Convention may be applicable and that the Convention governs and in most cases limits the liability of carriers for death or personal injury and in respect of loss or damage to baggage and cargo; Articles III:b), IV:b) and VII.

This means that the aircraft owner will be able, more frequently than now, to issue the documents in their required form. For, if the Protocol comes into force, it will no longer be necessary to set out the weight, the quantity, the volume or dimensions of the goods, or other particulars of the same kind. In consequence, the sanction—the loss of the liability limits—will seldom constitute an obstacle to the application of the Warsaw Rules and, in relation to passengers and shippers, the concept of carrier will correspond more closely to

[7] See *supra*, Ch. V (8).

the concept of operator, if the method of interpretation used in this study is accepted.

The discussions as to charter and hire at the Hague Conference did not result in any provision in the Protocol.[8] But the Final Act contains the following Recommendation (II:D):

"The Conference, having considered the report of the Sub-Committee of the Legal Committee of the International Civil Aviation Organization on the charter and hire of aircraft, and being of the opinion that the matter is of too great complexity to permit the insertion of provisions relating thereto in the Protocol to Amend the Warsaw Convention,

but considering that the matter is of considerable practical importance in view of the extent of charter and hire arrangements and requires further study,

recommends to the International Civil Aviation Organization that this subject should be further studied by the organization."

The author of this book sincerely hopes that his inquiries into the problem concerning the applicability of the Warsaw Convention to air charter may be found useful in the discussions that will take place as a result of this recommendation, and also that these discussions will finally reach their aim of finding an appropriate solution.

[8] Cf. *ibid.*, with footnote 14, and Riese, *Die internationale Luftprivatrechtskonferenz im Haag zur Revision des Warschauer Abkommens, September 1955*, Zeitschrift für Luftrecht 1956, pp. 4 et seq., on pp. 37–39.

APPENDICES

Appendix A. CONVENTION FOR THE UNIFICATION OF CERTAIN RULES RELATING TO INTERNATIONAL CARRIAGE BY AIR.

Warsaw 1929

(English translation from the original French text.)[1]

Chapter I. *Scope – Definitions*

ARTICLE 1.

(1) This Convention applies to all international carriage of persons, luggage or goods performed by aircraft for reward. It applies equally to gratuitous carriage by aircraft performed by an air transport undertaking.

(2) For the purposes of this Convention the expression "international carriage" means any carriage in which, according to the contract made by the parties, the place of departure and the place of destination, whether or not there be a break in the carriage or a transshipment, are situated either within the territories of two High Contracting Parties, or within the territory of a single High Contracting Party, if there is an agreed stopping place within a territory subject to the sovereignty, suzerainty, mandate or authority of another Power, even though that Power is not a party to this Convention. A carriage without such an agreed stopping place between territories subject to the sovereignty, suzerainty, mandate or authority of the same High Contracting Party is not deemed to be international for the purposes of this Convention.

[1] Cf. Drion, *Limitation of Liabilities in International Air Law,* The Hague 1954, pp. 346 et seq.

(3) A carriage to be performed by several successive air carriers is deemed, for the purposes of this Convention, to be one undivided carriage, if it has been regarded by the parties as a single operation, whether it had been agreed upon under the form of a single contract or of a series of contracts, and it does not lose its international character merely because one contract or a series of contracts is to be performed entirely within a territory subject to the sovereignty, suzerainty, mandate or authority of the same High Contracting Party.

ARTICLE 2.

(1) This Convention applies to carriage performed by the State or by legally constituted public bodies provided it falls within the conditions laid down in Article 1.

(2) This Convention does not apply to carriage performed under the terms of any international postal Convention.

Chapter II. *Documents of Carriage*

Section I: Passenger Ticket

ARTICLE 3.

(1) For the carriage of passengers the carrier must deliver a passenger ticket which shall contain the following particulars:—
   (a) the place and date of issue;
   (b) the place of departure and of destination;
   (c) the agreed stopping places, provided that the carrier may reserve the right to alter the stopping places in case of necessity, and that if he exercises that right, the alteration shall not have the effect of depriving the carriage of its international character;
   (d) the name and address of the carrier or carriers;
   (e) a statement that the carriage is subject to the rules relating to liability established by this Convention.

(2) The absence, irregularity or loss of the passenger ticket does not affect the existence or the validity of the contract of carriage, which shall none the less be subject to the rules of this Convention. Nevertheless, if the carrier accepts a passenger without a passenger ticket having been delivered he shall not be entitled to avail himself of those provisions of this Convention which exclude or limit his liability.

Section II: Luggage Ticket

ARTICLE 4.

(1) For the carriage of luggage, other than small personal objects of which the passenger takes charge himself, the carrier must deliver a luggage ticket.

(2) The luggage ticket shall be made out in duplicate, one part for the passenger and the other part for the carrier.

(3) The luggage ticket shall contain the following particulars:—

(a) the place and date of issue;

(b) the place of departure and of destination;

(c) the name and address of the carrier or carriers;

(d) the number of the passenger ticket;

(e) a statement that delivery of the luggage will be made to the bearer of the luggage ticket;

(f) the number and weight of the packages;

(g) the amount of the value declared in accordance with Article 22 (2);

(h) a statement that the carriage is subject to the rules relating to liability established by this Convention.

(4) The absence, irregularity or loss of the luggage ticket does not affect the existence or the validity of the contract of carriage, which shall none the less be subject to the rules of this Convention. Nevertheless, if the carrier accepts luggage without a luggage ticket having been delivered, or if the luggage ticket does not contain the particulars set out at (d), (f) and (h) above, the carrier shall not be entitled to avail himself of those provisions of the Convention which exclude or limit his liability.

Section III: Air Consignment Note

ARTICLE 5.

(1) Every carrier of goods has the right to require the consignor to make out and hand over to him a document called an "air consignment note"; every consignor has the right to require the carrier to accept this document.

(2) The absence, irregularity or loss of this document does not affect the existence or the validity of the contract of carriage which shall, subject to the provisions of Article 9, be none the less governed by the rules of this Convention.

ARTICLE 6.

(1) The air consignment note shall be made out by the consignor in three original parts and be handed over with the goods.

(2) The first part shall be marked "for the carrier", and shall be signed by the consignor. The second part shall be marked "for the consignee"; it shall be signed by the consignor and by the carrier and shall accompany the goods. The third part shall be signed by the carrier and handed by him to the consignor after the goods have been accepted.

(3) The carrier shall sign on acceptance of the goods.

(4) The signature of the carrier may be stamped; that of the consignor may be printed or stamped.

(5) If, at the request of the consignor, the carrier makes out the air consignment note, he shall be deemed, subject to proof to the contrary, to have done so on behalf of the consignor.

ARTICLE 7.

The carrier of goods has the right to require the consignor to make out separate consignment notes when there is more than one package.

ARTICLE 8.

The air consignment note shall contain the following particulars:—

(a) the place and date of its execution;

(b) the place of departure and of destination;

(c) the agreed stopping places, provided that the carrier may reserve the right to alter the stopping places in case of necessity, and that if he exercises that right the alteration shall not have the effect of depriving the carriage of its international character;

(d) the name and address of the consignor;

(e) the name and address of the first carrier;

(f) the name and address of the consignee, if the case so requires;

(g) the nature of the goods;

(h) the number of the packages, the method of packing and the particular marks or numbers upon them;

(i) the weight, the quantity, the volume or dimensions of the goods;[1]

(j) the apparent condition of the goods and of the packing;

(k) the freight, if it has been agreed upon, the date and place of payment, and the person who is to pay it;

(l) if the goods are sent for payment on delivery, the price of the goods, and, if the case so requires, the amount of the expenses incurred;

(m) the amount of the value declared in accordance with Article 22 (2);

(n) the number of parts of the air consignment note;

(o) the documents handed to the carrier to accompany the air consignment note;

(p) the time fixed for the completion of the carriage and a brief note of the route to be followed, if these matters have been agreed upon;

(q) a statement that the carriage is subject to the rules relating to liability established by this Convention.

[1] Cf. *supra*, Ch. IV (3), footnote 7.

9 – 565454 *Grönfors*

ARTICLE 9.

If the carrier accepts goods without an air consignment note having been made out, or if the air consignment note does not contain all the particulars set out in Article 8 (a) to (i) inclusive and (q), the carrier shall not be entitled to avail himself of the provisions of this Convention which exclude or limit his liability.

ARTICLE 10.

(1) The consignor is responsible for the correctness of the particulars and statements relating to the goods which he inserts in the air consignment note.

(2) The consignor will be liable for all damage suffered by the carrier or any other person by reason of the irregularity, incorrectness or incompleteness of the said particulars and statements.

ARTICLE 11.

(1) The air consignment note is *prima facie* evidence of the conclusion of the contract, of the receipt of the goods and of the conditions of carriage.

(2) The statements in the air consignment note relating to the weight, dimensions and packing of the goods, as well as those relating to the number of packages, are *prima facie* evidence of the facts stated; those relating to the quantity, volume and condition of the goods do not constitute evidence against the carrier except so far as they have been, and are stated in the air consignment note to have been, checked by him in the presence of the consignor or relate to the apparent condition of the goods.

ARTICLE 12.

(1) Subject to his liability to carry out all his obligations under the contract of carriage the consignor has the right to dispose

of the goods by withdrawing them at the aerodrome of departure or destination or by stopping them in the course of the journey on any landing or by calling for them to be delivered at the place of destination or in the course of the journey to a person other than the consignee named in the air consignment note or by requiring them to be returned to the aerodrome of departure. He must not exercise this right of disposition in such a way as to prejudice the carrier or other consignors and he must repay any expenses occasioned by the exercise of this right.

(2) If it is impossible to carry out the orders of the consignor the carrier must so inform him forthwith.

(3) If the carrier obeys the orders of the consignor for the disposition of the goods without requiring the production of the part of the air consignment note delivered to the latter, he will be liable, without prejudice to his right of recovery from the consignor, for any damage which may be caused thereby to any person who is lawfully in possession of that part of the air consignment note.

(4) The right conferred on the consignor ceases at the moment when that of the consignee begins in accordance with Article 13. Nevertheless, if the consignee declines to accept the consignment note or the goods, or if he cannot be communicated with, the consignor resumes his right of disposition.

ARTICLE 13.

(1) Except in the circumstances set out in the preceding Article, the consignee is entitled, on arrival of the goods at the place of destination, to require the carrier to hand over to him the air consignment note and to deliver the goods to him, on payment of the charges due and on complying with the conditions of carriage set out in the air consignment note.

(2) Unless it is otherwise agreed, it is the duty of the carrier to give notice to the consignee as soon as the goods arrive.

(3) If the carrier admits the loss of the goods, or if the goods have not arrived at the expiration of seven days after the date on which they ought to have arrived, the consignee is entitled to put into force against the carrier the rights which flow from the contract of carriage.

ARTICLE 14.

The consignor and the consignee can respectively enforce all the rights given them by Articles 12 and 13, each in his own name, whether he is acting in his own interest or in the interest of another, provided that he carries out the obligations imposed by the contract.

ARTICLE 15.

(1) Articles 12, 13 and 14 do not affect either the relations of the consignor or the consignee with each other or the mutual relations of third parties whose rights are derived either from the consignor or from the consignee.

(2) The provisions of Articles 12, 13 and 14 can only be varied by express provision in the air consignment note.

ARTICLE 16.

(1) The consignor must furnish such information and attach to the air consignment note such documents as are necessary to meet the formalities of customs, octroi or police before the goods can be delivered to the consignee. The consignor is liable to the carrier for any damage occasioned by the absence, insufficiency or irregularity of any such information or documents, unless the damage is due to the fault of the carrier or his agents.

(2) The carrier is under no obligation to enquire into the correctness or sufficiency of such information or documents.

Chapter III. *Liability of the Carrier*

ARTICLE 17.

The carrier is liable for damage sustained in the event of the death or wounding of a passenger or any other bodily injury suffered by a passenger, if the accident which caused the damage so sustained took place on board the aircraft or in the course of any of the operations of embarking or disembarking.

ARTICLE 18.

(1) The carrier is liable for damage sustained in the event of the destruction or loss of, or of damage to, any registered luggage or any goods, if the occurrence which caused the damage so sustained took place during the carriage by air.

(2) The carriage by air within the meaning of the preceding paragraph comprises the period during which the luggage or goods are in charge of the carrier, whether in an aerodrome or on board an aircraft, or, in the case of a landing outside an aerodrome, in any place whatsoever.

(3) The period of the carriage by air does not extend to any carriage by land, by sea or by river performed outside an aerodrome. If, however, such a carriage takes place in the performance of a contract for carriage by air, for the purpose of loading, delivery or trans-shipment, any damage is presumed, subject to proof to the contrary, to have been the result of an event which took place during the carriage by air.

ARTICLE 19.

The carrier is liable for damage occasioned by delay in the carriage by air of passengers, luggage or goods.

ARTICLE 20.

(1) The carrier is not liable if he proves that he and his agents have taken all necessary measures to avoid the damage or that it was impossible for him or them to take such measures.

(2) In the carriage of goods and luggage the carrier is not liable if he proves that the damage was occasioned by negligent pilotage or negligence in the handling of the aircraft or in navigation and that, in all other respects, he and his agents have taken all necessary measures to avoid the damage.

ARTICLE 21.

If the carrier proves that the damage was caused by or contributed to by the negligence of the injured person the Court may, in accordance with the provisions of its own law, exonerate the carrier wholly or partly from his liability.

ARTICLE 22.

(1) In the carriage of passengers the liability of the carrier for each passenger is limited to the sum of 125,000 francs. Where, in accordance with the law of the Court seised of the case, damages may be awarded in the form of periodical payments, the equivalent capital value of the said payments shall not exceed 125,000 francs. Nevertheless, by special contract, the carrier and the passenger may agree to a higher limit of liability.

(2) In the carriage of registered luggage and of goods, the liability of the carrier is limited to a sum of 250 francs per kilogram, unless the consignor has made, at the time when the package was handed over to the carrier, a special declaration of the value at delivery and has paid a supplementary sum if the case so requires. In that case the carrier will be liable to pay a sum not exceeding the declared sum, unless he proves that that sum is greater than the actual value to the consignor at delivery.

(3) As regards objects of which the passenger takes charge himself the liability of the carrier is limited to 5,000 francs per passenger.

(4) The sums mentioned above shall be deemed to refer to the French franc consisting of 65-½ milligrams gold of millesimal fineness 900. These sums may be converted into any national currency in round figures.

ARTICLE 23.

Any provision tending to relieve the carrier of liability or to fix a lower limit than that which is laid down in this Convention shall be null and void, but the nullity of any such provision does not involve the nullity of the whole contract, which shall remain subject to the provisions of this Convention.

ARTICLE 24.

(1) In the cases covered by Articles 18 and 19 any action for damages, however founded, can only be brought subject to the conditions and limits set out in this Convention.

(2) In the cases covered by Article 17 the provisions of the preceding paragraph also apply, without prejudice to the questions as to who are the persons who have the right to bring suit and what are their respective rights.

ARTICLE 25.

(1) The carrier shall not be entitled to avail himself of the provisions of this Convention which exclude or limit his liability, if the damage is caused by his wilful misconduct or by such default on his part as, in accordance with the law of the Court seised of the case, is considered to be equivalent to wilful misconduct.

(2) Similarly the carrier shall not be entitled to avail himself of the said provisions, if the damage is caused as aforesaid by any agent of the carrier acting within the scope of his employment.

ARTICLE 26.

(1) Receipt by the person entitled to delivery of luggage or goods without complaint is *prima facie* evidence that the same have been delivered in good condition and in accordance with the document of carriage.

(2) In the case of damage, the person entitled to delivery must complain to the carrier forthwith after the discovery of the damage, and, at the latest, within three days from the date of receipt in the case of luggage and seven days from the date of receipt in the case of goods. In the case of delay the complaint must be made at the latest within fourteen days from the date on which the luggage or goods have been placed at his disposal.

(3) Every complaint must be made in writing upon the document of carriage or by separate notice in writing despatched within the times aforesaid.

(4) Failing complaint within the times aforesaid, no action shall lie against the carrier, save in the case of fraud on his part.

ARTICLE 27.

In the case of the death of the person liable, an action for damages lies in accordance with the terms of this Convention against those legally representing his estate.

ARTICLE 28.

(1) An action for damages must be brought, at the option of the plaintiff, in the territory of one of the High Contracting Parties, either before the Court having jurisdiction where the carrier is ordinarily resident, or has his principal place of business, or has an establishment by which the contract has been made or before the Court having jurisdiction at the place of destination.

(2) Questions of procedure shall be governed by the law of the Court seised of the case.

ARTICLE 29.

(1) The right to damages shall be extinguished if an action is not brought within two years, reckoned from the date of arrival at the destination, or from the date on which the aircraft ought to have arrived, or from the date on which the carriage stopped.

(2) The method of calculating the period of limitation shall be determined by the law of the Court seised of the case.

ARTICLE 30.

(1) In the case of carriage to be performed by various successive carriers and falling within the definition set out in the third paragraph of Article 1, each carrier who accepts passengers, luggage or goods is subjected to the rules set out in this Convention, and is deemed to be one of the contracting parties to the contract of carriage in so far as the contract deals with that part of the carriage which is performed under his supervision.

(2) In the case of carriage of this nature, the passenger or his representative can take action only against the carrier who performed the carriage during which the accident or the delay occurred, save in the case where, by express agreement, the first carrier has assumed liability for the whole journey.

(3) As regards luggage or goods, the passenger or consignor will have a right of action against the first carrier, and the passenger or consignee who is entitled to delivery will have a right of action against the last carrier, and further, each may take action against the carrier who performed the carriage during which the destruction, loss, damage or delay took place. These carriers will be jointly and severally liable to the passenger or to the consignor and the consignee.

Chapter IV. *Provisions relating to Combined Carriage*

ARTICLE 31.

(1) In the case of combined carriage performed partly by air and partly by any other mode of carriage, the provisions of this Convention apply only to the carriage by air, provided that the carriage by air falls within the terms of Article 1.

(2) Nothing in this Convention shall prevent the parties in the case of combined carriage from inserting in the document of air carriage conditions relating to other modes of carriage, provided that the provisions of this Convention are observed as regards the carriage by air.

Chapter V. *General and Final Provisions*

ARTICLE 32.

Any clause contained in the contract and all special agreements entered into before the damage occurred by which the parties purport to infringe the rules laid down by this Convention, whether by deciding the law to be applied, or by altering the rules as to jurisdiction, shall be null and void. Nevertheless for the carriage of goods arbitration clauses are allowed, subject to this Convention, if the arbitration is to take place within one of the jurisdictions referred to in the first paragraph of Article 28.

ARTICLE 33.

Nothing contained in this Convention shall prevent the carrier either from refusing to enter into any contract of carriage, or from making regulations which do not conflict with the provisions of this Convention.

ARTICLE 34.

This Convention does not apply to international carriage by air performed by way of experimental trial by air navigation undertakings with the view to the establishment of a regular line of air navigation, nor does it apply to carriage performed in extraordinary circumstances outside the normal scope of an air carrier's business.

ARTICLE 35.

The expression "days" when used in this Convention means current days, not working days.

ARTICLE 36.

The Convention is drawn up in French in a single copy which shall remain deposited in the archives of the Ministry for Foreign Affairs of Poland and of which one duly certified copy shall be sent by the Polish Government to the Government of each of the High Contracting Parties.

ARTICLE 37.

(1) This Convention shall be ratified. The instruments of ratification shall be deposited in the archives of the Ministry for Foreign Affairs of Poland, which will notify the deposit to the Government of each of the High Contracting Parties.

(2) As soon as this Convention shall have been ratified by five of the High Contracting Parties it shall come into force as between them on the ninetieth day after the deposit of the fifth ratification. Thereafter it shall come into force between the High Contracting Parties who shall have ratified and the High Contracting Party who deposits his instrument of ratification on the ninetieth day after the deposit.

(3) It shall be the duty of the Government of the Republic of Poland to notify to the Government of each of the High Contracting Parties the date on which this Convention comes into force as well as the date of the deposit of each ratification.

ARTICLE 38.

(1) This Convention shall, after it has come into force, remain open for accession by any State.

(2) The accession shall be effected by a notification addressed to the Government of the Republic of Poland, which will inform the Government of each of the High Contracting Parties thereof.

(3) The accession shall take effect as from the ninetieth day after the notification made to the Government of the Republic of Poland.

ARTICLE 39.

(1) Any one of the High Contracting Parties may denounce this Convention by a notification addressed to the Government of the Republic of Poland, which will at once inform the Government of each of the High Contracting Parties.

(2) Denunciation shall take effect six months after the notification of denunciation, and shall operate only as regards the Party who shall have proceeded to denunciation.

ARTICLE 40.

(1) Any High Contracting Party may, at the time of signature or of deposit of ratification or of accession declare that the acceptance which he gives to this Convention does not apply to all or any of his colonies, protectorates, territories under mandate, or any other territory subject to his sovereignty or his authority, or any territory under his suzerainty.

(2) Accordingly any High Contracting Party may subsequently accede separately in the name of all or any of his colonies, protectorates, territories under mandate or any other territory subject to his sovereignty or to his authority or any territory under his suzerainty which has been thus excluded by his original declaration.

(3) Any High Contracting Party may denounce this Convention, in accordance with its provisions, separately or for all or any of his colonies, protectorates, territories under mandate or any other territory subject to his sovereignty or to his authority, or any other territory under his suzerainty.

ARTICLE 41.

Any High Contracting Party shall be entitled not earlier than two years after the coming into force of this Convention to call for the assembling of a new international Conference in order to consider any improvements which may be made in this Convention. To this end he will communicate with the Government of the French Republic which will take the necessary measures to make preparations for such Conference.

This Convention done at Warsaw on the 12th October, 1929, shall remain open for signature until the 31st January, 1930.

Additional Protocol

(with reference to Article 2)

The High Contracting Parties reserve to themselves the right to declare at the time of ratification or of accession that the first paragraph of Article 2 of this Convention shall not apply to international carriage by air performed directly by the State, its colonies, protectorates or mandated territories or by any other territory under its sovereignty, suzerainty or authority.

Appendix B. EXTRACTS FROM THE IATA "RESOLUTION 045" CONCERNING THE RESALE OF CHARTERED SPACE.

1 (b) Charter agreements shall be made with only one person (which expression shall include persons, associations, partnerships, companies, corporations or other legal entities) for his own use; provided that charter agreements may be made with one person on behalf of a group, whose principal aims, purposes and objectives are other than travel and where the group has sufficient affinity existing prior to the application for charter transportation to distinguish it and set it apart from the general public, but any such charter agreement shall contain a stipulation that the charterer will not permit the aircraft to be used by any person other than himself or a member of such group;

1 (c) charter agreements for passengers shall contain a stipulation by the charterer on his own behalf and of anyone deriving rights from him, that they will not sell directly or indirectly any of the chartered space; provided that this shall not preclude re-sale of space within a group as defined in sub-paragraph (b) above;

1 (d) charter agreements for cargo shall contain a stipulation by the charterer, on his behalf and on behalf of anyone deriving rights from him, that they will not sell directly or indirectly any chartered space; provided that this shall not preclude re-sale of space with a definitely recognisable group (e.g. farmers);

1 (e) charter agreements shall contain a warranty by the charterer that he has not already held out and will not hold out by advertisement, course of conduct or other means, individual passages to the public generally for transportation on the charter trip. A reference in any public advertising or publicity to the amount being charged per person shall be deemed to be such a holding out;

(2) Notwithstanding the foregoing, no charter agreement shall be made directly or indirectly with persons engaged;

(a) In providing surface carriage, except that the charter agreements may be made with such persons for carriage (i) of their own personnel and property and (ii) of their passengers, baggage and cargo; provided that the charter carriage is necessitated by an emergency and the charterer does not demand or receive, from the passengers and shippers, any compensation over and above that paid or payable in respect of the surface carriage for which the air carriage is substituted, and provided further it is understood that agents of shipping companies shall be entitled to charter aircraft for the movement of crews of one or more vessels or companies; each charter agreement entered into pursuant to this sub-paragraph shall contain an appropriate stipulation setting forth the conditions herein provided.

(b) in soliciting carriage; except that an agent shall not be precluded from signing a charter agreement on behalf of a person or group as specified in sub-paragraph (1) (b).